HANK WILLIAMS
The Singer and the Songs

Don Cusic

Books by Don Cusic

Eddy Arnold: His Life and Times (2016)

The Beatles and Country Music (2015)

James Weldon Johnson: Songwriter (2013)

Roger Miller: Dang Him (2012)

Elvis and Nashville (2012)

Dressed in Grey & Blue (Novel) (2012)

Sharecropper's Son (Novel) (2011)

The Cowboy in Country Music (2011)

Encyclopedia of Contemporary Christian Music (Editor) (2010)

The Trials of Henry Flipper: First Black Graduate of West Point (2009)

Discovering Country Music (2008)

Gene Autry: His Life and Career (2007)

Johnny Cash: The Songs (2004)

Baseball and Country Music (2003)

It's the Cowboy Way: The Amazing True Adventures of Riders In The Sky (2003)

Merle Haggard: Poet of the Common Man (2002)

Saved By Song: A History of Gospel and Christian Music (2002)

Eddy Arnold: I'll Hold You in My Heart (1997)

Music in the Market (1996)

Willie Nelson: Lyrics 1957-1994 (1995)

Cowboys and the Wild West: An A-Z Guide From the Chisholm Trail to the Silver Screen (1994)

Hank Williams: The Complete Lyrics (1993)

The Poet As Performer (1991)

Reba: Country Music's Queen (1991)

Randy Travis: The King of the New Country Traditionalists (1990)

Sandi Patti: The Voice of Gospel (1988)

Hank Williams: Poet

CHAPTER

1

If you want to define country music, just listen to a recording of Hank Williams singing. There is no denial there, no threat of crossover or urban identity crisis, no complexities that confuse the listener. This is country music and Hank Williams remains the master.

It was Hank who established the prototype, the stereotype of the country music singer songwriter. It was Hank who personified the image of the tortured genius. His shadow still looms over the world of country music and his ghost still haunts the singers and songwriters who inhabit that world. In his time he was a superstar and many years after his death he is still a superstar, a contemporary figure, an influence, a legend, a mystery, and a force to be reckoned with. Hank Williams is the songwriter against whom every other country songwriter is measured.

Shining through it all are his songs, the living monuments of Hank Williams that have never tarnished. Hank Williams is still the greatest songwriter in country music. His songs are not the slickly contrived ditties from Tim Pan Alley or the product of a committee of songwriters on Music Row; they are raw genius, ragged nerves, pure emotion bursting through in a simplicity that captured a complex man. The songs are timeless, hits years ago and hits today when artists record them. They are a magnet, attracting the best singers to sing them and the best writers who try and capture what Hank seemed to do without trying. Or maybe what Hank couldn't help doing--writing masterpieces in simple verse and chorus format. It is the songs that have defied mortality, that continue to live on, long after the singer is gone. It is his songs that reveal the man, define country music, and make the man immortal. They are a goal to be aimed at, striven for. They continue to make Hank Williams larger than life, always alive.

His story is a rags to riches saga, complete with a tragic ending. In his life are all the elements of drama and in his songs the drama is played out. Hank Williams did not just live, he exploded and tiny sparks of his light still shine on. His life is the story behind the songs.

CHAPTER

2

Hank Williams was born "King Hiram Williams" on September 17, 1923 in Mt. Olive, Alabama; his parents, Elonzo H. and Lillian (Skipper) Williams named him after biblical King Hiram in the Book of Kings. They had one other child, a daughter Irene, who was 13 months older. As a boy, Hank lived in the Georgiana area in Butler County in the towns of Mt. Olive, Garland, Chapman, Ruthven Mill and McWilliams. In 1935 the family moved to Greenville where his musical talent grew and developed and in 1937, when Hank was around 13, to Montgomery, where he launched his professional career.

Hank's father, Lon Williams, entered a V.A. Hospital in 1930 and stayed there for the next 10 years, leaving Hank to grow up without the benefit of a father's influence and leaving Hank's mother, Lilly--a strong and domineering woman--to head the household. Lilly Williams made her living by running a boarding house, supplementing her income by raising vegetables, strawberries and working at the WPA cannery in Montgomery. Hank hustled on the streets and earned money for himself and his family by selling peanuts, shining shoes, delivering groceries, running errands and other odd jobs. Although the family was relatively poor, they did not seem to want for the basics of food and clothing.

The first strong musical influence on Hank was a black street singer named Tee-tot (real name: Rufus Payne). Hank not only learned chords on the guitar and songs from Tee-tot, but also a bit of showmanship. Tee-tot coached Hank with his music as Hank tried some street singing himself.

Hank's first stage success came in 1937 at the Montgomery Empire Theatre where he sang during one of the original amateur nights and won first prize. The song he sang, "W.P.A. Blues," patterned after the song "Dissatisfied," is believed to be his first original composition. Later, he played over WSFA, a 1,000 watt station in Montgomery, appearing twice weekly for fifteen minute shows. His shows were a local success; he formed his first band, The Drifting Cowboys, when he was 13 years old. He kept this name for his band his entire professional career.

At the age of 18, Hank met Audrey Mae Sheppard at a medicine show in Banks, Alabama, where Hank was the singer and salesman. They were married on a Saturday night, December 15, 1944, at a rural filling station in Andalusia, Alabama. She had been married to a local man, Erskine Guy, and had a daughter Lycrecia. Hank and Audrey were married ten days after her divorce became final, although a 30 day waiting period was required by Alabama law. For the eight years they were married, she was the greatest single personal influence in his life, the inspiration for a number of songs, and, to his death, a presence and force he could never escape.

Two strong women dominated Hank's life, his mother, Lillian and his wife, Audrey. Both were instrumental in his professional career as well as his personal life.

Wesley Rose, who worked with Hank as a publisher, has stated, "You could tell how things were going at home by what Hank was writing." The couple's relationship consisted of a constant round of fighting, then making up, according to insiders, and the success Hank achieved as well as his own personal problems from back pain, with booze, being on the road and the increasing demands of being in the public spotlight amplified their problems and made solutions impossible.

Although Hank was widely known for his attraction to the "sporting life," Audrey remained his true love. On the road, Hank regularly kept company with other females but Audrey held the strings to his heart. It is impossible to dissect or explain why she had such influence on Hank; suffice it to say that he was simply in love with her.

Audrey was an attractive woman with blonde wavy hair, a long face with prominent nose and mouth, tall and six months older than Hank. Within her she carried the ambition that was a root cause for Hank Williams being successful as well as a major reason his life was difficult.

After their marriage, Audrey quickly became a member of Hank's group, assuming some of Lilly's tasks like booking shows, collecting tickets and taking care of the finances. She sang--albeit poorly--and could play a little guitar. She was a stabilizing force and made sure the Drifting Cowboys covered a date when Hank failed to appear. According to Roger Williams, in his biography, *Sing a Sad Song*, "Sex aside, Hank and Audrey had a ragged, sometimes tempestuous relationship. Each was headstrong and, in their own distinct way, talented. Each had personality traits that rubbed the other the wrong way. Hank was tense inside but easygoing on the surface; except in moments of self-pitying bitterness, he was not aggressive, and he was not really ambitious in the materialistic sense."

Hank and Audrey were often in conflict because she was acquisitive and socially ambitious, which was aggravated by Hank's chronic back pain (probably from spina bifida) and alcoholism, which steadily worsened as his fame grew. In many ways, Hank was a weak man and avoided responsibility, which led to Audrey being the mate, a mirror of Hank's parents relationship of the weak male dominated by a strong woman.

Roger Williams states, "Some interpreters of the Williams marriage have played to the hilt Audrey's roles as a catalyst in the creation of Hank's songs...People like to think it literally created them, but it did not. The songs were the product of his genius, which would have been present had he been the happiest man in the world. Neurotic conflict of the type that afflicted Hank can enhance and concretize creativity, but the creativity is not a product of the conflict."

CHAPTER

3

Hank was a "star" in Montgomery from his appearances on WSFA and his ability to draw a crowd at local clubs. While most country artists moved from city to city for radio exposure and to reach a newer and wider audience for their personal appearances, Hank remained in Montgomery until after his professional career was established.

During his early years in Montgomery, Hank had recorded several songs that indicate his influences. He recorded the song "Happy Roving Cowboy," written by Bob Nolan and recorded by the Sons of the Pioneers. Hank was not a "western" singer but he dressed like one and this song influenced his look more than his sound. Hank loved the singing cowboy movies that were popular during the 1930s; Gene Autry, Roy Rogers and Tex Ritter starred in a number of those while the Sons of the Pioneers sang in many of those movies. The songs of the Sons of the Pioneers reflect a strong, three (and sometimes four) part harmony. Hank's songs were for the single voice, although there might be harmony singing on the chorus, but the sound of vocal harmonies was never part of Hank's sound.

During the early 1940s, before Hank signed with Acuff-Rose Publishing in Nashville, he also recorded "Freight Train Blues," a traditional song done by Roy Acuff, "San Antonio Rose" by Bob

Wills" and "I Ain't Gonna Love You Any More" by Ernest Tubb in Montgomery.

A song that Hank wrote, "I'm Not Coming Home Anymore," was recorded as a guitar/vocal demo in April, 1942 at the Highland Bridge Radio and Shoe Shop.

CHAPTER

4

ank's professional career received its biggest boost in September, 1946, when he and Audrey went to Nashville in search of Fred Rose, head of Acuff-Rose, at that time a relatively young publishing company that dealt almost exclusively with country music.

Wesley Rose, son of Fred Rose and later head of the publishing conglomerate--now one of the largest in the world--told of the meeting with Hank this way. "My father and I were playing ping pong at WSM. It was just before noon when this tall, skinny guy and his wife--you could tell they were country--walked up and she asked if her husband could sing some of his songs. My father looked at me and said, 'Have we got time?' and I looked at my watch and said 'Sure,' so the four of us went into one of the studios and Hank sang six songs he had written. The songs were 'Calling You,' 'Six More Miles,' 'Never Again Will I Knock On Your Door,' 'Wealth Won't Save Your Soul,' 'When God Comes and Gathers His Jewels,' and 'My Love For You Has Turned To Hate.'" Rose added that the often repeated story that Hank was given a "test" to see if he had written the songs--and coming up with "Mansion On The Hill" was not true.

After Hank had sung those six songs, Fred Rose took him to the Acuff-Rose offices, which were located in the WSM building, and signed him to a songwriters' contract.

However, in the biography of Hank Williams by Colin Escott with George Merritt and William MacEwen, a different story emerges. It is "almost certain that Hank wasn't making a cold call, that Wesley wasn't there and that 'Mansion on the Hill' wasn't written until a year later," wrote Escott, who asserts that on Saturday, September 14, 1946 when Hank and Audrey took the train to Nashville to meet with Fred Rose, it was "by invitation."

Acuff-Rose was a publishing company and Fred Rose sought songs and songwriters to sign to the publishing company. Rose also found artists to produce with Acuff-Rose as a source of songs. Molly O'Day (born Lois LaVerne Williamson) was a well-respected singer during the 1940s who had appeared on West Virginia radio stations WCHS in Charleston, WJLS in Beckley and WHIS in Bluefield. She married guitarist Lynn Davis in 1941 and the two performed together on radio stations and on appearances in Birmingham, Louisville and Renfro Valley, Kentucky before they joined the "Mid-Day Merry-Go-Round" on WNOX in Knoxville in May, 1945.

Fred Rose recommended that Art Satherley, head of country A&R for Columbia Records, sign O'Day and he did; Rose would produce her recordings. Rose had heard her sing "Tramp On The Street"—her most popular number—and asked where she found the song. She told him that she heard Hank Williams sing it in Montgomery during an appearance there. Lynn Davis, who was aware that Hank wrote songs, suggested that Rose contact Hank and Rose wrote him a letter, inviting him to Nashville.

Fred Rose was probably aware of Hank Williams because Pee Wee King, who was signed as a songwriter to Acuff-Rose (King and Redd Stewart wrote "Tennessee Waltz") had purchased a song from Hank, "(I'm Praying For the Day That) Peace Will Come" which was published by Acuff-Rose.

In 1943—during World War II—Pee Wee King did a tour of Alabama and Hank Williams was also booked on that tour. Hank pitched "(I'm Praying for the Day That) Peace Will Come" to Pee Wee after singer Becky Barfield said she needed another patriotic number. According to Colin Escott, King and Barfield were apprehensive but Hank encouraged them to try the song in front of an audience and it apparently went over well. King then purchased the rights to the song from Hank with a contract written out by hand. There are several stories of where this happened; in one version, the song was purchased for $50 while the troupe was at the Municipal Auditorium in Montgomery while another story states the agreement was made in Dothan, Alabama.

King took the song to Fred Rose in Nashville for Acuff-Rose Publishing and the copyright was registered with the Library of Congress on December 20, 1943. King did not obtain a recording contract until 1945—the year the war ended—so he never recorded it. After World War II there was no demand for patriotic wartime songs until the Korean War in 1950, when Rosco Hankins (real name: Esco Hankins) recorded it for Mercury. The song did not chart.

CHAPTER

5

Fred Rose would emerge as the most important professional influence in Hank Williams' life. A successful pop songwriter before he became a country music publisher, Rose had written songs like "Red Hot Mama," "Honest and Truly," and "Deed I Do" before he turned his attention to country. He was born August 24, 1897 in Evansville, Indiana and was a child prodigy, becoming an accomplished pianist by the age of ten, a professional musician by thirteen and, at seventeen, began his songwriting career in Chicago. In addition to writing in the Tin Pan Alley vein during the 1920's, he also performed as pianist with Paul Whiteman's Orchestra and on radio with Elmo Tanner, eventually obtaining his own fifteen-minute radio show on the CBS network from the WBBM studio in Chicago.

When the Depression hit in the 1930's, Rose's rosy days ended and he began job-hopping from city to city, eventually coming to Nashville in 1933 to work on WSM. He returned to Chicago for a short while before coming back to Nashville in 1935, writing country songs. He then moved to New York where he met singing cowboy Ray Whitley and they co-wrote several hits for Gene Autry, including "Ages and Ages Ago," "Lonely River," and "I Hang My Head And Cry." Alone, Rose composed "Tears On My Pillow," "Tweedle-O-Twill," "Rainbow On The Rio Colorado" and

"Be Honest With Me" for Autry; the latter song was nominated for an Academy Award in 1942.(It lost to "White Christmas" by Irving Berlin from the film, *Holiday Inn*.)

During World War II, when Gene Autry enlisted in the Army Air Corps, Rose returned to Nashville as a successful country songwriter and wrote "Fireball Mail," "Low And Lonely," and "Pins and Needles In My Heart" for Roy Acuff. Acuff and Rose went into the publishing business together in 1943, forming the company that would grow to be an international publishing giant and the home of Hank Williams' songs.

Beginning in the mid-1940's, when Rose was approaching fifty, he began his most productive output as a songwriter, penning "Deep Water" and "Roly Poly" for Bob Wills, "At Mail Call Today" for Gene Autry, "It's a Sin" for Eddy Arnold and, in the 1950's, "Foggy River" for Carl Smith and "Kaw-Liga" for Hank Williams as well as "Blue Eyes Crying In The Rain," which became a hit for Willie Nelson in the 1970's.

One of Rose's greatest attributes was finding and encouraging talent in others. In addition to Hank Williams, Rose helped develop the songwriting talents of Pee Wee King and Redd Stewart, the Louvin Brothers, Jenny Lou Carson, and Felice and Boudleaux Bryant.

Rose's relationship with Hank Williams was both personal and professional. "He was like a father to Hank," stated Wesley Rose, and provided the young uneducated singer necessary advice and guidance. Professionally, he controlled Hank's record releases, deciding when a record would be released, what markets would be targeted, and which songs would be promoted as well as re-writing, editing, shaping and polishing Hank's songs.

Hank Williams' songs would not have been as commercially successful without the input of Fred Rose, although Hanks' natural genius provided the raw material. It is safe to say that Hank provided rough diamonds that Rose cut and polished; the raw genius belonged to Hank but the craftsmanship of shaping and molding the songs belonged to Rose, who often did not take credit for his efforts. According to Roger Williams, "In truth, the Rose contribution varied widely from song to song, because the condition of the material varied widely. Hank's songs reached Rose in all sorts of stages, from complete lyrics and melody to half verses and a rough outline to a chorus and no melody to nothing but a theme or an idea. Rose, who was one of the slickest, most professional songwriters in the history of American popular music, took each song or germ of a song and did what had to be done... (his) most frequent contribution was smoothing out Hank's lyrics, adding a word or a phrase that brought the song alive."

According to Colin Escott, "Rose deliberately excluded everyone from his writing sessions with Hank, so we'll never know who did precisely what, but in all likelihood Rose brought no more than a commercial gloss and organizational skills to Hank's work. He encouraged him to write bridges rather than simply string verses together and provided a much needed element of quality control."

"Hank did most of his writing on the road," continued Escott. "There wasn't even room to break out a guitar in the sedan, so he'd beat out a rhythm on the dashboard and someone would get something like a cardboard stiffener from a pressed shirt and take the words down. Hank would come back off the road with a billfold full of scraps of paper on which he had verses, half completed songs, and abandoned ideas…All the melodies were in Hank's head…It was up to Fred Rose to separate the wheat from the chaff and to work with Hank to make integrated, complete songs taut with rigid commercial logic. If Rose contributed substantially, as he did on 'Mansion on the Hill' and later 'Kaw-Liga,' he took half the credit; if he simply doctored a song up, he didn't."

Roy Acuff stated, "They worked as a good team of mules. They pulled right together. Hank would come up with the ideas, and Fred would say, 'Well, write it down and let me look at it.' Hank'd bring it to Fred, and Fred would sit at the piano and complement Hank and say, 'Well, maybe you ought to express this a little differently. Let's change it a little bit,' but Fred never changed Hank's thinking."

After Hank met with Fred Rose in Nashville in September, 1946, he went back to Montgomery and recorded vocal/guitar demos of "You Broke Your Own Heart," "A House of Gold," "Pan American," "Wealth Won't Save Your Soul" and "Calling You."

Hank had self-published two songbooks in Montgomery in 1945 and 1946 before he met Fred Rose and many of his early songs were in those songbooks. "Honky Tonkin'" was in his first song folio as "Honkey-Tonkey."

CHAPTER

6

During the Fall of 1946, Fred Rose was contacted by Al Middleman with Sterling Records, headquartered in New York. The label was a small independent backed by investors which had a jazz, pop and rhythm & blues series and wanted to expand into black gospel and country music. Rose agreed to find acts for Sterling, record them and ship the masters to New York. The agreement was for the acts to be signed to short-term contracts that offered only a fee for the recordings with no royalties.

Rose first contacted Johnnie and Jack, but they were with the Apollo label. Rose then signed the Oklahoma Wranglers, a group formed by the Willis brothers in 1932. Guy Willis played guitar, Skeeter the fiddle and Vic the accordion. After military service during World War II, the Willis brothers reunited and added Chuck "The Indian" Wright on bass.

The Oklahoma Wranglers had sent a demo recording to Harry Stone with WSM which resulted in an invitation to debut on the Grand Ole Opry in June, 1946 and perform on the Checkerboard Jamboree, sponsored by Purina and starring Eddy Arnold and Ernest Tubb.

On the morning of December 11, 1946, the Willis group arrived at the WSM Studio on the corner of Seventh Avenue North and Union. That morning they rehearsed Hank's songs with him, had lunch at the nearby Clarkston Hotel, and that afternoon Hank had his first professional recording session backed by the Oklahoma Wranglers.

The first song recorded on Hank's session was "Calling You," a gospel number. This was followed by "Never Again (Will I Knock On Your Door)" the only secular number on the session, then "Wealth Won't Save Your Soul" and "When God Comes and Gathers His Jewels." All of the songs were written by Hank and published by Acuff-Rose.

"Calling You" was released in January, 1947, billed as "Hank Williams with the Country Boys" with "Never Again (Will I Knock On Your Door) on the "B" side. The release was advertised in *Billboard* by Sterling, which announced "a new Hillbilly series." The advertisement noted that "For singing real country songs Hank Williams is tops. He's a big favorite wherever he's heard and this record will sell like hot cakes." Neither side of the record charted.

Hank's second single for Sterling "Wealth Won't Save Your Soul" backed with "When God Comes and Gathers His Jewels" was released in February, 1947.

After Hank's first session, he recorded two songs as vocal/guitar demos in Montgomery, "You Broke Your Own Heart" and "I'm So Tired of It All."

CHAPTER

7

Hank's next professional recording session occurred on February 13, 1947 at the WSM Studios in Nashville, once again for Sterling. The Willis brothers were unavailable (they had signed with Mercury) so Fred Rose hired WSM staff musicians Tommy Jackson (fiddle), Dale "Smokey" Lohman (steel guitar), Zeke Turner (electric guitar) and Louis Innis (bass). Hank recorded "I Don't Care (If Tomorrow Never Comes)," "Honky Tonkin'," "My Love For You (Has Turned To Hate)" and "Pan American."

"Pan American" was about the Pan American Clipper, who's whistle was broadcast every day over WSM; it was a train on the Louisville and Nashville line. Hank used the melody of "Wabash Cannon Ball," credited to A.P. Carter of The Carter Family but actually written by J.A. Roff. Hank used a lot of old melodies—and some by contemporary writers—in many of his songs.

The third single Hank released on Sterling was "I Don't Care (If Tomorrow Never Comes)" with "My Love For You (Has Turned To Hate)" on the "B" side; this was released in March, 1947—the third straight month a single by Hank was released. Neither side charted.

The fourth, and last, single released by Sterling was "Honky Tonkin'" with "Pan American" on the "B" side. It was released in May, 1947 but neither side charted, although "Honky Tonkin'" would later be a hit.

CHAPTER

8

Hanks' third professional recording session occurred on April 21, 1947 at the Castle Studio in Nashville. Castle was Nashville's first major professional recording studio. The Castle Recording Laboratories, as the facility was officially known, was started by three WSM radio engineers, Aaron Shelton, Carl Jenkins and George Reynolds; the name came from the WSM logo, "Air Castle of the South."

At first, the engineers used the WSM Studio in the old National Life Building then, because of increasing work, rented space in the Tulane Hotel on Church Street between Seventh and Eighth Avenues north.

The agreement with Sterling had ended and Fred signed Hank to MGM Records, headed by Frank Walker after Art Satherley with Columbia and Steve Sholes with RCA Victor had both turned down Hank. Walker was a veteran in the recording industry; he had signed Bessie Smith when he was at Columbia, where he created their Blues and Hillbilly series. He had also signed early country artists Riley Puckett, Gid Tanner, Charlie Poole and Clarence "Tom" Ashley. He then joined RCA and during World War II was involved with the V Disk program. After the War, he re-joined RCA and signed Eddy Arnold. He was recruited by MGM to start their record division, which began in March, 1947. MGM was a new label with strong financial backing; Hank Williams would give them a new country artist. The contract was signed on April 1, 1947.

Walker had already signed pop acts Jimmy Dorsey, Kate Smith, Ziggy Elman and Billy Eckstine and country acts Sam Nichols, the Korn Kobblers and Carson Robison. The agreement between Walker and Rose called for Rose to receive no fee for producing and a lower publishing rate for sales but Rose would use Acuff-Rose copyrights as much as possible.

Accompanying Hank on the session were Nashville musicians Tommy Jackson on fiddle, Dale "Smokey" Lohman on steel guitar, Zeke Turner on electric guitar, Louis Innis on rhythm guitar and Bronson "Brownie" Reynolds on bass. In the studio they recorded "Move It On Over," "I Saw the Light," "(Last Night) I Heard You Cryin' In Your Sleep" and "Six More Miles (to the Graveyard)."

"Move It On Over" was Hank's first chart record; it was released on June 6, 1947 and reached number four on the country chart. On the "B" side was "(Last Night) I Heard You Cryin' In Your Sleep." It was Hank's fifth single.

"I Saw the Light" with "Six More Miles (To the Graveyard)" was not released until September 24, 1948; it was Hank's eleventh single and did not chart.

CHAPTER

9

On August 4, 1947 at the Castle Studio, accompanied by his Alabama band, L.C. Crysel (fiddle), Sammy Pruett (lead guitar), Herman Herron (steel guitar), Slim Thomas (rhythm guitar) and Lum York (bass), Hank began the session with "Fly Trouble," a song written by the Jamup and Honey team of Honey Wilds and Lasses White with Fred Rose. The next songs were, in order, "Honky Tonk Blues," "I'm Satisfied With You" (written by Fred Rose) and "On the Banks of the Old Pontchartrain," which is credited to Hank and Ramona Vincent. Kathleen Ramona Vincent had sent the lyric to Hank, who put a melody to the lyrics. Vincent was a crippled lady, probably from Louisiana.

The first single released from that session was "Fly Trouble" with "On The Banks of the Old Ponchartrain" on the "B" side; it was released on September 26, 1947 but did not chart. "Fly Trouble" seems an odd choice for Hank to record. It is a novelty song, more reminiscent of Western Swing than the honky tonk sound Hank was suited for and probably done because Rose thought this novelty type song (reminiscent of Rose's "Roly Poly") would be popular on jukeboxes. "I'm Satisfied With You" was not released until after Hank's death and Hank's version of "Honky Tonk Blues" on this session was never released.

Fred Rose was dissatisfied with Hank's band and aborted the session, which is why those versions of "I'm Satisfied With You" and "Honky Tonk Blues" were never released.

By the end of 1947 MGM had a strong line-up of artists with Bob Wills, Denver Darling, Rome Johnson, and Carson Robison on the label. Their biggest hit that year was Carson Robison's "Life Gits Tee-Jus, Don't It."

CHAPTER

10

There was a musicians strike, called by James Caesar Petrillo, head of the American Federation of Musicians, set to begin on January 1, 1948 so Fred Rose and Hank Williams went into the Castle studio and recorded seven songs over two days, November 6 and 7. Musicians were Chubby Wise on fiddle, Jerry Byrd on steel guitar, Zeke Turner on electric guitar, probably Louis Innis on bass and either Fred Rose or Owen Bradley on piano. Hank wanted to use his own band again but instead Fred hired Chubby Wise, the fiddler for Bill Monroe and the Bluegrass Boys, and Red Foley band members Byrd and Clements.

On Hank's session on November 6, 1947 he recorded "Rootie Tootie," "I Can't Get You Off of My Mind," "I'm a Long Gone Daddy" and "Honky Tonkin.'" On November 7 they recorded "My Sweet Love Ain't Around," "The Blues Come Around," "A Mansion on the Hill" and "I'll Be a Bachelor 'Till I Die."

The first single from those sessions was "Rootie Tootie," written by Fred Rose, and once again Rose had Hank record a novelty-type song, similar to "Fly Trouble," "Roly Poly," or even "Deed I Do." Once again, it didn't work. It was Hank's seventh single, with "My Sweet Love Ain't Around" on the "B" side. Released on January 2, 1948, neither side charted.

Fred had recorded "Rootie Tootie" on Pee Wee King and Opry western swing artist Paul Howard and all three versions were released in January, 1948. None of them charted, but Pee Wee King's version was on the back of "Tennessee Waltz," a song he wrote with Redd Stewart.

The next single was "Honky Tonkin'," which was Hank's second chart single. It was released on April 9, 1948 and reached number 14 on *Billboard's* country chart. It was backed by "I'll Be a Bachelor 'Til I Die." The third single from those sessions was "I'm a Long Gone Daddy," released on June 18, 1948. It was Hank's third chart single (it reached number six) with "The Blues Come Around" on the "B" side. That single was released on June 18, 1948.

Since the recording strike had not ended by mid-1948, MGM went back to some of the songs from Hank's Sterling sessions and released "Pan American" with "I Don't Care (If Tomorrow Ever Comes)" on July 16, 1948 and "I Saw the Light" with "Six More Miles (To the Graveyard)" on the "B" side on September 24, 1948. None of those songs charted.

The recording strike ended in early December and on the last day of 1948 MGM released "Mansion on the Hill" with "I Can't Get You Off of My Mind" on the "B" side.

A story circulated for years that during his initial meeting with Hank in September, 1946, Fred told Hank to "prove" he had written the songs he had played for Rose by going into a room and writing a song. That did not happen. What did happen was that Rose gave Hank a title, "Mansion on the Hill," and told him to write a song when he went back to Montgomery.

According to Audrey Williams, as related in Colin Escott's book, "Fred said...'To prove to me you can write, I'm gonna give you a title, and I want you to take it back to Montgomery and write a song around it.' Hank worked with it and worked with it, but he never could do too much good with it, and the reason he couldn't was because it wasn't his idea. One night I had just finished with the dinner dishes, and I started singing 'Tonight down here in the valley..' After I got through with it, I took it in to Hank and said, 'Hank, what do you think of this?' He really liked it, and it was a mixture of my lyrics, Hank's lyrics, and Fred Rose's lyrics. Hank sent it in, and for a long time I wouldn't tell anybody that I had anything to do with that because I wanted it to be all Hank."

According to Colin Escott, "The reason Hank had a problem with 'Mansion on the Hill' was that he was very weak at writing narrative ballads. All of his best songs were interior snapshots." The melody to "Mansion on the Hill" came from "I Wonder If You Feel The Way I Do," a song recorded by Bob Wills in 1938. The melody may have been in the Public Domain.

All of those songs were released on 78 rpm records although some were later released as a 45 rpm single.

"Mansion on the Hill" was released on December 31, 1948; it was the twelfth single by Hank and reached number 12 on the *Billboard* country chart; however, it did not chart until after his next release, "Lovesick Blues," was a hit. The "B" side was "I Can't Get You Off of My Mind."

CHAPTER

11

While Hank lived in Montgomery during 1947 and 1948, he recorded a number of vocal/guitar demos to send to Fred Rose. Those songs were for Fred Rose to listen to and decide whether they would be recorded by Hank or pitched to other artists to record. Those songs were "Won't You Sometimes Think of Me," "Why Should I Cry?," "I Watched My Dream World Crumble Like Clay," "I Told a Lie to My Heart," "Mother is Gone," "In My Dreams You Still Belong to Me," "Calling You," "Honky Tonk Blues," "A Home in Heaven," "I'm Going Home" and "Singin' Waterfall."

All of the songs were released after Hank died. This recording of "Honky Tonk Blues" was released in 1985. The recordings of "I'm Going Home," "Singin' Waterfall," "Won't You Sometimes Think of Me," "Why Should I Cry?" "I Watched My Dream World Crumble Like Clay," "I Told a Lie To My Heart," and "In My Dreams You Still Belong To Me" were not released until 1986 on the album *The First Recordings* on the Country Music Foundation's label; in 1998 most were released in the boxed set *The Complete Hank Williams*.

Hank also recorded a demo (that didn't survive) of "If I Didn't Love You," which he wrote with Fred Rose. It was recorded by Rome Johnson on November 25, 1947.

CHAPTER

12

By the summer of 1948 Hank had released three records that charted. "Move It On Over" had entered the chart in 1947 and risen to number four. "Honky Tonkin'" and "I'm a Long Gone Daddy" both entered the chart in July, 1948; "I'm a Long Gone Daddy" reached number six and "Honky Tonkin'" got to number 14, but they didn't remain on the chart for long; only three weeks for "I'm a Long Gone Daddy" and one week for "Honky Tonkin.'"

Hank needed to leave Montgomery for something bigger, but he wasn't quite big enough for the Grand Ole Opry. Also, despite the influence of Fred Rose, the Opry brass had heard of Hank's problems with booze and unreliability and were reluctant to commit to him. It was wait and see time for the Opry and Hank; meanwhile, Fred Rose negotiated for Hank to appear on the Louisiana Hayride in Shreveport—just a notch down from the Opry in terms of country music radio shows.

In June, Fred Rose bought the Sterling Masters of Hank's early recordings, then sold them to MGM.

Hank Williams arrived in Shreveport, Louisiana to join the Louisiana Hayride on KWKH in August, 1948. The Louisiana Hayride was a live country music radio show which served as a sort of "farm club" for the Opry during the late 40's and early 50's.

A number of singers, including Jim Reeves, Webb Pierce, Elvis Presley, The Browns, Johnny Horton, Slim Whitman, Johnnie and Jack and Kitty Wells and musicians such as Jerry Kennedy, D.J. Fontana James Burton and Floyd Cramer, first obtained important exposure on the Shreveport show.

The Louisiana Hayride was only four months old when Hank joined. KWKH was founded in 1922 and had an early "Saturday Night Roundup" show that was discontinued during World War II. After the War, the owners hired Horace Logan as program director and disc jockey. Logan was inspired to start the Louisiana Hayride after a visit to the Grand Ole Opry and he patterned the Hayride after the Opry.

Hank realized the importance of doing well there, so he cut out his drinking and curbed the boozing, unreliable reputation he had acquired in Montgomery. During the time he was in Shreveport, Hank made trips to Nashville to record under the production of Fred Rose.

Perhaps the most significant event to occur in the life of Hank Williams while he was living in Shreveport was the birth of his son, Randall Hank, on May 26, 1949. Known today as Hank Williams, Jr., he has firmly established himself as a star in country music through his own talents.

CHAPTER

13

In late fall, 1948, Hank recorded two vocal/guitar demos in Shreveport, "Dear Brother" (accompanied by Johnnie Wright and Kitty Wells on vocals) and "Time Has Proven I Was Wrong." "Dear Brother is credited to Hank and Juanita Acuff. "Time Has Proven I Was Wrong" is credited to Hank, Mel Foree and Curley Williams. Both of those recordings were first released in 1998 on the boxed set, *The Complete Hank Williams*.

Curley Williams and his band, The Peach Pickers, were members of the Grand Ole Opry during World War II and recorded for Columbia Records. Curley and his group went to the West Coast in 1945 to play dances, then moved to Shreveport in 1948 to play on the Hayride. During 1948, Hank and Audrey lived with Curley and his wife, Louise, for a time.

Mel Foree was the promotion man for Acuff-Rose, which promoted their songs by sending sheet music and records of Acuff-Rose songs that had been recorded to radio station D.J.'s. In the Fall of 1948, Fred Rose sent Foree to Shreveport to help promote Hank. Hank and Foree traveled on the road together and wrote four songs, which Hank recorded as vocal/guitar demos and sent them to Fred Rose. All of the songs were written to a melody Hank had already used so the only salvageable one was "'Neath a Cold Gray Tomb of Stone."

Hank never recorded that song for MGM but Charlie Monroe, brother of Bill Monroe, recorded it in October, 1950.

Back in Shreveport, Hank, Foree and Curley Williams wrote two songs, "No, Not Now," which Curley recorded in September, 1949, and "Time Has Proven I Was Wrong."

CHAPTER

14

The song which launched Hank Williams into the national spotlight and onto the stage of the Grand Ole Opry was "Lovesick Blues," a number he did not write. It seems ironic that Williams, known for his songwriting, received his big break from an old pop tune that had been around for close to thirty years. Hank recorded "Lovesick Blues" in Cincinnati on December 22, 1948, shortly after the musician's strike had been resolved.

E.T. Herzog had established his recording studio at 811 Race Street in Cincinnati in 1945. Herzog, an engineer with WLW, recorded the earliest releases on King Records before King established their own studio. Herzog's studio had excellent recording facilities and a number of country sessions were held there before he closed shop in 1951. Hank's session was set there because Red Foley's former band members had moved to Cincinnati after being offered more money than they we remaking on WSM. They performed as "The Pleasant Valley Boys" on WLW and "The Midwestern Hayride."

Musicians on the session were Tommy Jackson, fiddle; Jerry Byrd, steel guitar; Zeke Turner, electric guitar; Louis Innis, rhythm guitar; Clyde Baum, mandolin and Willie Thawl (an announcer at WLW) on bass.

Fred had set the session to record new releases for MGM. Hank had sent demos of the songs he wanted to record to Fred, who only found one song he liked, "There'll Be No Teardrops Tonight." That song had WLW disc jockey Nelson King credited as co-writer. King, one of the most powerful disc jockeys in country music, had received co-writing credit on another song ("Three Ways of Knowing" by Johnnie and Jack) because of his importance in breaking records.

Country artists often called disc jockeys to plug their records and Hank had often called King to promote his. Somewhere along the line, Hank apparently got drunk and cut King in on "There'll Be No Teardrops Tonight."

Two songs on the session, "Lost On The River' and "I Heard My Mother Praying For Me" were duets with Audrey; the first song was written by Hank and the second song was written by Audrey. The group recorded "There'll Be No Teardrops Tonight" and finished with about a half an hour left on the session.

Hank had performed on shows with Rex Griffin, who had recorded "Lovesick Blues" and was aware of the version by Emmett Miller. The song was an old Broadway song written by Irving Mills and Cliff Friend for the show, "O-oo Ernest." It was originally recorded in 1922, but Emmett Miller introduced a yodel into the song when he performed it as a blackface routine. Rex Griffin had recorded the song in 1939.

Hank had performed "Lovesick Blues" in Montgomery and on the Louisiana Hayride in Shreveport and saw the crowd response to the song, which led him to want to record it. Hank recorded a demo of the song and sent it to Rose, but Rose wrote back saying he didn't want anything to do with it.

When Hank pulled the song out at the end of the session, Fred Rose reportedly told him, "That's the worst damn thing I ever heard." Fred made it clear he didn't want Hank to record it but Hank was determined, telling Rose, "You might not like the song but when it gets so hot that I walk off the stage and throw my hat back on the stage and the hat encores, that's pretty hot."

Disgusted, Fred walked out of the session to get a cup of coffee, telling the musicians he would pay them time and a half if they finished before the three hours were up.

The song had originally begun with "I'm in love, I'm in love" as the verse with "I've got a feeling called the blues" as the chorus. In running down the song, the musicians, desperate to come up with a workable arrangement in a short time, switched the verse and chorus.

The musicians did not like the song either and, in fact, most of the professional musicians on Hank's early recordings did not like his singing or songs. He was "too country." There had long been a bias against country music within the country music establishment; even many of the players and performers looked down on the music.

Searching for an intro to the song, Jerry Byrd and Zeke Turner decided to use an intro they had recorded for Ernest Tubb's record of the Jimmie Rodgers song, "Waitin' For a Train." For that song, the musicians simulated the Rodgers yodel for the intro and they did the same thing for "Lovesick Blues." After two takes, the session was over.

Hank told Fred that the song was written by Rex Griffin and Acuff-Rose could have the publishing. Rose filed the paperwork for the song giving Griffin songwriting credit and naming Acuff-Rose as the publisher.

The first single released from this session was "Lovesick Blues" with a song from the Sterling sessions, "Never Again (Will I Knock On Your Door)" on the "B" side. It was released on a 78 rpm record on February 11, 1949 and entered the *Billboard* chart on March 5. It raced to number one on the chart and remained there for 16 consecutive weeks, remaining on the chart for 42 weeks. This was Hank's thirteenth single and is the song that made Hank Williams a star; without "Lovesick Blues," there would not be the Hank Williams that we know today.

The flip side, "Never Again (Will I Knock On Your Door)" also made the *Billboard* chart, staying only two weeks but reaching number six.

When "Lovesick Blues" hit, Irving Mills sued. Frank Walker, head of MGM, had to step in and sort out the negotiations. It was agreed that Acuff-Rose would share the publishing for Hank's version only because of the promotion done by Acuff-Rose. The royalties for the song would be split between the two publishers but all future recordings of the song would be published by Mills.

"Mansion On the Hill," which was released on the last day of 1948, benefitted from the popularity of "Lovesick Blues." It entered the *Billboard* chart the same week as "Lovesick Blues," and spent two weeks on the chart, reaching number twelve.

"Lost on the River" was on the "B" side of "Dear Brother," released as Hank and Audrey on May 17, 1949. It did not chart.

"There'll Be No Tear Drops Tonight" was released on July 15, 1949 as the "B" side of "Mind Your Own Business." Although the "A" side charted, the "B" side did not.

CHAPTER

15

etween August, 1948, when Hank moved to Shreveport, until May, 1949, when he moved to Nashville, Hank recorded a number of vocal/guitar demos. Those songs were written by Hank and sent to Fred Rose, who determined which songs Hank would record, which he would pitch to other artists, and which he felt were not commercial enough to be recorded.

Those songs were "A House of Gold," "Singin' Waterfall," "Heaven Holds All My Treasures," "Lost on the River," "Honey Do You Love Me, Huh?" (credited to Hank and Curley Williams), "'Neath a Cold Gray Tomb of Stone (credited to Hank and Mel Foree), "No, Not Now" (credited to Hank with Mel Foree and Curley Williams) and "When You're Tired of Breakin' Other Hearts" (credited to Hank and Curley Williams).

Only two of the songs by Hank, "Lost on the River" and "A House of Gold," was released during Hank's lifetime ("House of Gold" was released on an album in June, 1952). Hank's version of "Singin' Waterfall" was released in 1956. "No, Not Now" was released in the U.K. on an album in 1981. Two others were not released until 1985 when the Country Music Foundation released the album, *Just Me and My Guitar* that contained "Heaven Holds All of My Treasure" and "Lost On the River." "'Neath a Cold Gray Tomb of Stone" was released in 1985 on the album *Hank Williams On The Air* and "Honey, Do You Love Me, Huh?" was released in 1998 on the box set *The Complete Hank Williams*. "When You're Tired of Breakin' Other Hearts" was never issued.

A demo of "You're Barking Up the Wrong Tree Now," which has been lost, was also recorded by Hank. The song was written with Fred Rose and was recorded by Red Sovine on September 1, 1949.

Sometime during 1948 Hank and Audrey recorded a demo of a song written by A.P. Carter, "Something Got a Hold of Me."

CHAPTER

16

Horace Logan, the program director of KWKH, gave Hank a 15 minute morning show (times varied when on the air between 5:30 a.m. and 8 a.m.) sponsored by Johnnie Fair Syrup beginning in January, 1948. (Hank called himself "The Ole Syrup Sopper.") If Hank had to be away from the station for personal appearances, he recorded programs on transcription discs in the KWKH studio that could be used. On the show he sang songs (without a band) and made pitches for the syrup. During the period between January and May, 1949, he recorded a number of songs for the show, most of them made famous by other artists. He only recorded one original, "Alone and Forsaken."

The songs he recorded (with the writer(s) listed) were: "Please Don't Let Me Love You" (Ralph Jones), "Faded Love and Winter Roses" (Fred Rose), "First Year Blues" (Ernest Tubb), "There's No Room in My Heart For the Blues" (Fred Rose and Zeb Turner), "Rock My Cradle (Once Again)" (Johnny Bond and Billy Folger), "Little Paper Boy" (Jim Anglin and Johnnie Wright), "I Wish I Had a Nickel" (W.S. Barnhart and Tommy Sutton), "Rockin' Chair Money" (Lonnie Glosson and Bill Carlisle), "Tennessee Border" (Jimmie Work), "My Main Trial is Yet to Come" (Pee Wee King and J.L. Frank), "The Devil's Train" (Mel Foree and Cliff Carlisle), "Cool Water" (Bob Nolan), "The Waltz of the Wind" (Fred Rose), "At the First Fall of Snow" (Lorene Rose), "Dixie Cannonball" (Gene Autry,

Red Foley and Vaughn Horton), "I'm Free At Last" (Ernest Tubb), "You Caused It All By Telling Lies" (Clyde Moody), "Leave Me Alone With the Blues" (Joe Pope), "It Just Don't Matter Now" (Ernest Tubb), "Swing Wide Your Gate of Love" (Hank Thompson), "We Planted Roses on My Darling's Grave" (Roy Acuff and Odel MacLeod), "The Old Home" (Jackie Earls), "Sundown and Sorrow" (Pee Wee King), "The Prodigal Son" (Floyd Jenkins, the pseudonym of Fred Rose), "A Tramp On The Street" (Grady Cole and Hazel Cole), "Someday You'll Call My Name" (Eddie Hill and Jean Branch), "Thank God" (Fred Rose), "Blue Love (In My Heart)" (Floyd Jenkins/Fred Rose), "Roly Poly" (Fred Rose), "The Battle of Armageddon" (Roy Acuff and Odel MacLeod), "We Live in Two Different Worlds" (Fred Rose), "Wait For the Light to Shine" (Fred Rose), "No One Will Ever Know" (Mel Foree and Fred Rose), "With Tears In My Eyes" (Paul Howard) and "Don't Do It Darling" (Zeke Manners).

"Alone and Forsaken" is unique because it is in a minor key and Hank rarely wrote in a minor key. In fact, other than "Kaw-Liga," which starts in a minor key, "Alone and Forsaken" is Hank's only minor key song.

The acetates of those songs from the KWKH studio that Hank recorded with just his guitar were left in Shreveport until the mid-1950s when a disc jockey on KWKH found them. Leonard Chess, owner of Chess Records in Chicago, bought them from the DJ and then sold them to MGM.

Chess Records was known as a blues label; they had Chuck Berry, Muddy Waters, Bo Diddley, Howlin' Wolf, Etta James and other R&B greats, but during the 1950s some R&B labels attempted to branch out into country music, which is probably why Leonard Chess bought them.

CHAPTER

17

Why did Hank Williams, one of the greatest—if not THE greatest songwriter of all time—sing songs written by other people? It's simple. Hank Williams was an entertainer as well as a songwriter and a songwriter has to perform songs that people recognize and like. An audience wants to hear hits and many of the songs Hank sang on the Johnny Fair show were hits.

A number of those songs were published by Acuff-Rose so Fred Rose may have encouraged Hank to "try them out." Rose would not have wanted Hank to be singing any songs that weren't copyrighted by Acuff-Rose, so that was another reason to perform songs from other performers on the radio station.

Hank Williams wasn't just a consummate songwriter, he was also a consummate performer who had an impact on an audience. At that point in his career, Hank did not have many proven hits to sing and, in fact, a number of his releases had not been played enough on jukeboxes or on radio for audiences to be familiar with them. A performer needs to entertain a crowd and, if the singer has not written enough hits for an evening's performance, then he must find songs elsewhere.

During his time in Shreveport Hank recorded two vocal/ guitar demos in Nashville of "We're Getting Closer to the Grave Each Day" and "The Alabama Waltz."

CHAPTER

18

On March 1, 1949—a little over two weeks after "Lovesick Blues" had been released and four days before it entered *Billboard's* country chart, Hank was in the Castle Studio in Nashville for back-to-back sessions that started at 7:30 in the evening and did not finish until 2 a.m. on the morning of March 2.

Backed by musicians Dale Potter on fiddle, Don Davis on steel guitar, Zeb Turner on electric guitar, Jack Shook on rhythm guitar, Clyde Baum on mandolin and probably Ernie Newton on bass, Hank recorded four songs on the first session that ended at 10:30 p.m., "Dear Brother," "Jesus Remembered Me," "Lost Highway" and "May You Never Be Alone."

"Dear Brother" was a duet with Hank and Audrey; it was released as a single on May 17, 1940 (issued as "Hank and Audrey") with their duet of "Lost On the River" on the "B" side. It did not chart.

"Jesus Remembered Me" was also a duet by Hank and Audrey. It was not released until October 6, 1950 as the "B" side of "I Heard My Mother Praying For Me," Hank's twenty-sixth single. It was released as "Hank and Audrey".

"Lost Highway" was written by Leon Payne, a blind musician from Houston, Texas who performed at a club there. Payne had originally recorded the song in October, 1948, for Bullet Records, an independent label established in Nashville. Payne also wrote the classic, "I Love You Because."

"Lost Highway" is a country classic and many believe Hank wrote it. The song was released on September 9, 1949 as the "B" side of "You're Gonna Change (Or I'm Gonna Leave)," Hank's seventeenth single. That record was a two sided hit with "Lost Highway" reaching number 12 on the country chart.

The final song on the session, "May You Never Be Alone" was released on January 27, 1950 as the "B" side of "I Just Don't Like This Kind of Livin.'" "May You Never Be Alone" is another classic Hank song, but it never charted. It was first released on a 78 rpm record in 1949 and then issued on a 45 rpm in 1950.

After a half hour break, the musicians resumed recording at 11 p.m. with "Honky Tonk Blues," then "Mind Your Own Business," "You're Gonna Change (Or I'm Gonna Leave)" and "My Son Calls Another Man Daddy."

"Mind Your Own Business," Hank's sixteenth single, was released on July 15, 1949 and reached number five on the country chart; the "B" side was "There'll Be No Teardrops Tonight," which did not chart. It followed the single "Dear Brother" backed with "Lost On The River" released as "Hank and Audrey." "Lovesick Blues" was still on the chart when this record was released and joined Hank's hit on the chart and reached number five. The "B" side was "There'll Be No Teardrops Tonight."

That single was followed by "You're Gonna Change (Or I'm Gonna Leave")" which was a two-sided hit; it reached number four on the country chart and the "B" side was "Lost Highway," which reached number 12.

Hank's recording of "My Son Calls Another Man Daddy," credited to Hank and Jewell House, was not released; apparently Fred Rose was not satisfied with the recording but Hank liked the song and would record it again on a session nine months later. The original version of "My Son Calls Another Man Daddy" and "Honky Tonk Blues" were not released until 1984 when they were on the album *Rare Takes and Radio Cuts*.

CHAPTER

19

Less than three weeks later, on an evening session on March 20, 1949 at the Castle Studio, Hank recorded "Wedding Bells," "I've Just Told Mama Goodbye," "I'm Going Home" and "We're Getting Closer to the Grave Each Day."

On this session he was backed by Dale Potter on fiddle, Don Davis on steel guitar, Zeb Turner on electric guitar, Jack Shook on rhythm guitar and Velma Williams on bass. "Wedding Bells," credited to Claude Boone, was actually written by James Arthur Pritchett, who performed locally in Knoxville as Arthur Q. Smith. Smith is an interesting story in the history of country music. He was a down and out alcoholic who often wrote songs and sold them for $15-25. These were not ordinary songs; Smith supposedly wrote—and sold—the Ernest Tubb hit "Rainbow at Midnight," "If Teardrops Were Pennies," which was a hit for Rosemary Clooney and "I Wouldn't Change You If I Could," which became a hit for Ricky Skaggs. "Wedding Bells" was originally recorded by Bill Carlisle in 1947 after it had been purchased by Boone, who was a guitarist in the bluegrass band of Carl Story.

"Wedding Bells" was released on May 6, 1949, the follow-up single to "Lovesick Blues" and reached number two on the country chart. The "B" side was "I've Just Told Mama Goodbye," which was written by Slim Sweet and Curley Kinsey.

On April 4, Molly O'Day recorded "On the Evening Train," a song written by Audrey that Hank recorded as a duet with Audrey.

In the summer of 1949 Hank recorded a duet of "When You're Tired of Breaking Others' Heart," written with Curley Williams; this song was recorded by Curley Williams on September 15, 1952.

CHAPTER

20

"Lovesick Blues" was voted "Best Hillbilly Record" of the year in *Cashbox* and was voted number one in *Billboard's* listing of the top country and western records for 1949.

With "Lovesick Blues" exploding across the country over radio, on juke boxes and over-the-counter store sales, WSM general manager Harry Stone arranged a guest appearance for Hank on the Grand Ole Opry on June 11, 1949. Hank was introduced by Red Foley on his Opry debut. Most of the audience there knew "Lovesick Blues" but did not know Hank. According to legend, Hank had to do six encores before he was allowed to leave--and then only because Red Foley insisted the show go on; however, a recording of the Hank's performance shows that he only sang the song once.

After this--and because he had stayed sober for two years in Shreveport--Hank Williams was set to join the Grand Ole Opry.

Hank moved to Nashville and the Grand Ole Opry in the summer of 1949. In addition to belonging to the Opry, he appeared on several radio shows at WSM, the station that owned the Opry, and was booked by the Opry Artists' Bureau for personal appearances during the week.

When he moved to Nashville, Hank assembled the Drifting Cowboy's band that was to back him on the personal appearances and recordings. The band consisted of Bob McNett on lead guitar, Don Helms on steel guitar, Hillous Butrum on bass and Jerry Rivers playing fiddle. Hank also developed his team on the business side. It consisted of Fred Rose, his publisher and confidant; Sam Hunt, an executive for Third National Bank who handled Hank's money; and Jim Denny, general manager of the Opry and head of the Opry Artists' Bureau that booked Hank. Denny was also a friend and confidant.

CHAPTER

21

"I'm So Lonesome I Could Cry" is considered a classic Hank Williams song, perhaps his most poetic. Ironically, it was not a hit during his lifetime and it was not until 1966 when it was re-released with new backing that it became a chart record for Hank, but it only reached number 43 that summer and stayed on the chart just four weeks. (It had been a pop hit for B.J. Thomas earlier that year.)

"I'm So Lonesome I Could Cry" was the first song recorded by Hank on his session at the E.T. Herzog Studio in Cincinnati on August 30, 1949, two and a half months after he joined the Grand Ole Opry and around the time he moved from Shreveport to Nashville.

Hank was backed on this session by Tommy Jackson on fiddle, Jerry Byrd on steel guitar, Zeke Turner on electric guitar, Louis Innis on rhythm guitar and Ernie Newton on bass during an afternoon session that started at 2 and finished at 5 p.m. Dissatisfied with the quality of Hank's previous band, Fred went to Cincinnati to record with Red Foley's former band members.

"I'm So Lonesome I Could Cry" was originally written as a spoken word song, but Hank decided to sing it, borrowing the title from another song released by MGM. After recording "I'm So Lonesome I Could Cry," the next songs recorded were "A House

Without Love," "I Just Don't Like This Kind of Livin'" and "My Bucket's Got a Hole in It," which was credited to Clarence Williams.

"My Bucket's Got a Hole in It" was Hank's eighteenth single, released on November 18, 1949 with "I'm So Lonesome I Could Cry" on the "B" side. "My Bucket's Got a Hole in It" entered the *Billboard* chart on November 26 and reached number two.

"A House Without Love" was the "B" side of "Why Don't You Love Me," Hank's twenty-second single and did not chart.

"I Just Don't Like This Kind of Livin'" was Hank's nineteenth single; it was released on January 27, 1950 and reached number five on the country chart; it was the fourth consecutive single by Hank to reach the charts. The "B" side was "May You Never Be Alone."

During 1949, after Hank moved to Nashville, he recorded three songs as vocal/guitar demos, "'Neath a Cold Gray Tomb of Stone," written with Mel Foree, was recorded by Charlie Monroe on October 20, 1949. "No, Not Now," written with Curley Williams and Mel Foree, was recorded by Curley Williams on September 11, 1949. "Jesus Died For Me" was recorded by Roy Acuff in December, 1949.

CHAPTER

22

In October, 1949, Hank spent two days in the Castle Recording Studio recording eight "Health and Happiness" shows. The 15-minute shows were intended for broadcast and came about because Matt Hedrick, advertising manager of WSM, had approached Dudley J. LeBlanc, founder of the tonic Hadacol to sponsor Hank. Hadacol was a popular tonic that was laced with alcohol and "guaranteed to cure your ills." "Hadacol Boogie" by Bill Nettles had been a big hit and LeBlanc wanted Hank on his traveling medicine shows to promote the tonic.

Hank did not mention Hadacol on the show; instead, he made a generic pitch to stay tuned for an important message from the D.J. Those recordings were the first made by Hank's Drifting Cowboy Band, which had only been together for three months.

Songs on those shows demonstrate the material Hank was singing during his live appearances. His theme song was "Happy Roving Cowboy" and he started each show with that number. There were instrumentals, usually by fiddler Jerry Rivers, of traditional fiddle tunes "Sally Goodin,'" "Old Joe Clark," "Fire On the Mountain," "Bill Cheatam," "Bile Them Cabbage Down," "Fingers of Fire" (played by guitarist Bob McNett), "Wagner," "Arkansas Traveler," "Cotton-Eyed Joe" and "Fisherman's Hornpipe."

There were songs by other writers: "Wedding Bells," "Where the Soul of Man Never Dies" (Wayne Raney), "A Tramp On The Street" (Grady Cole-Hazel Cole), "Lost Highway" (Leon Payne), "I Want To Live and Love Always" (Gene Sullivan-Wiley Walker), "I'll Have a New Body (I'll Have a New Life)" (Luther G. Presley), "The Prodigal Son" (by Fred Rose under the name Floyd Jenkins)," "I've Just Told Mama Goodbye" (Slim Sweet-Curley Kinsey) and "Thy Burden's Are Greater Than Mine" (Pee Wee King-Redd Stewart) and his big hit, "Lovesick Blues" (Cliff Friend-Irving Mills).

There were songs sung by Audrey, "(There's a) Bluebird On Your Windowsill" (Elizabeth Clarke-Robert Mellin) and "I'm Telling You."

Finally, there were Hank's originals: "You're Gonna Change (Or I'm Gonna Leave)," "I'm a Long Gone Daddy," "A Mansion On the Hill," "There'll Be No Teardrops Tonight," "Pan American," "I Saw the Light," "Mind Your Own Business," "I Can't Get You Off of My Mind" and "I'm So Lonesome I Could Cry."

CHAPTER

23

Hank Williams broke through as a major star in country music during 1949. During that year he had eight songs on the *Billboard* country chart: "Mansion On the Hill," "Lovesick Blues," "Never Again (Will I Knock On Your Door)," "Wedding Bells," "Mind Your Own Business," "You're Gonna Change (Or I'm Gonna Leave,)" "Lost Highway" and "My Bucket's Got a Hole in It."

This was the beginning of Hank's brightest stardom during his life--from June 1949 until August, 1952. He became the biggest, brightest star in country music, and a songwriter whose works propelled his own career as well as numerous others. The groundwork was laid during this time for Hank Williams to become the most influential artist and songwriter in the history of country music.

With Fred Rose living nearby and Hank visiting the Acuff-Rose offices nearly every day he was in town, his songwriting fully developed and blossomed. That development of his songwriting came from being around other professionals as well being coached by Rose as Hank nurtured his own genius.

After the move to Nashville, it was also the time of a stable, happy home life. At first, Hank did not let booze get in the way of his career. In fact, for about two years he did not enter any hospitals or sanitariums to combat alcoholism--the only time in his life he went that long without entering those institutions. Hank Williams knew that his career depended on him staying sober so he did. Above all, he was ambitious and on the way up the ladder he wanted nothing in his way to stop his climb. It was only after he had become a phenomenal success and had to face the demands of stardom did he resume his heavy drinking and let it become a problem that would ruin his life.

CHAPTER

24

Hank recorded four songs during an afternoon session at Castle Studio on January 9, 1950. The songs were "Long Gone Lonesome Blues," "Why Don't You Love Me?," "Why Should We Try Anymore?" and "My Son Calls Another Man Daddy." Frank Walker, head of MGM Records, was in the studio for this session.

By this time, Hank had a solid line-up of Drifting Cowboys and they backed him on this session. Bob McNett played electric guitar, Don Helms played steel guitar and Jerry Rivers played fiddle; they were joined by Nashville musicians Jack Shook on rhythm and Ernie Newton on bass.

Since "Lovesick Blues" had been a major hit, Hank wanted another song where his voice broke into a semi-yodel and he found it in "Long Gone Lonesome Blues." Vic McAlpin often told the story of going fishing with Hank and Hank had not gotten his line overboard so McAlpin asked, "Are you going to fish or just watch 'em swim by?" "That's it!" replied Hank and he sang the opening line, "I went down to the river to watch the fish swim by." McAlpin claimed he wrote the song with Hank and that Hank sent him money when royalties for that song came in, but McAlpin's name is not on that song.

Two and a half months later, on March 10, "Long Gone Lonesome Blues" was released and became Hank's twenty-first single; on the "B" side was "My Son Calls Another Man Daddy." "Long Gone Lonesome Blues" was a number one record for Hank, remaining in that position for eight consecutive weeks and 21 weeks on the chart. "My Son Calls Another Man Daddy" reached number nine on the chart.

The follow-up single to "Long Gone Lonesome Blues" was "Why Don't You Love Me?," released on May 19 and it also reached number one, remaining in that position for ten weeks and stayed on the chart for 25 weeks. "A House Without Love" was on the "B" side (it did not chart).

"Why Should We Try Anymore" was on the "B" side of "They'll Never Take Her Love From Me," released on August 18, 1950. "Why Should We Try Anymore" reached number nine on the country chart in *Billboard*.

CHAPTER

25

The day after Hank recorded "Long Gone Lonesome Blues" and "Why Don't You Love Me," he recorded four songs as "Luke the Drifter." These were spoken word recitations with an instrumental background. Hank had wanted to record recitations but Fred Rose resisted; Hank's market was jukeboxes and his singles were aimed at the jukebox market but jukeboxes did not want to program sad recitations so MGM released the records under the name, "Luke the Drifter" for the "take home" market (songs consumers would purchase to play at home).

There was never any secret that "Luke the Drifter" was Hank Williams but if the records were released as "Hank Williams" the jukebox operators would order in bulk and then have a large supply left over. So, to make it easier and more convenient, Hank recorded his recitations as "Luke the Drifter."

There's a long history of recitations in country music. In 1948, two years before Hank's "Luke the Drifter" sessions, T. Texas Tyler had a big hit with "Deck of Cards."

On the afternoon of January 10, 1950, starting at 2 p.m. Hank recorded "Too Many Parties and Too Many Pals" (written by Billy Rose, Mort Dixon and Ray Henderson), "Beyond the Sunset" (written by Blanche Kerr Brock, Virgil P. Brock and Albert Kennedy Rowswell), "The Funeral"(credited to Hank but the lyrics were by Will Carlton from a poem he wrote in 1909) and "Everything's OK." These were mostly proven songs. T. Texas Tyler and Elton Britt had both recorded "Beyond The Sunset" and Tyler had recorded "The Funeral" (as "The Colored Child's Funeral"). Bill Haley had recorded "Too Many Parties."

Hank was backed on the session by Don Helms on steel guitar, Hillous Butrum on bass with either Fred Rose or Owen Bradley on organ.

"The Funeral" was released a month later, on February 10, with "Beyond the Sunset" on the "B" side. This was the first single Hank released as "Luke the Drifter."

"Everything's OK" was Hank's second Luke the Drifter single, released on June 16 with "Too Many Parties and Too Many Pals" on the "B" side. Since none of the Luke the Drifter singles were sent to radio, none of them charted because the charts were compiled from jukebox airplay.

Billboard introduced its country singles chart as "Juke Box Folk Records" on January 8, 1944. From 1944 until May 8, 1948, the charts were compiled from jukebox sales and play. Beginning Mary 15, 1948, *Billboard* added another country singles chart, "Best Selling Retail Folk Records" and on December 10, 1949 a third country singles chart, "Most Played by Folk Disk Jockeys" was introduced. The "Juke Box" chart ended on June 17, 1957. Hank's earliest "chart" records were compiled from jukebox sales and play. His releases after December, 1949 incorporated airplay on radio.

CHAPTER

26

Hank's wife, Audrey, wanted to record with Hank and sing on his programs; unfortunately, she was not a great singer. This caused Hank problems as well as problems for Fred Rose, who managed to obtain a recording contract for Audrey with Decca Records, headed by Paul Cohen with Owen Bradley assisting during the recording sessions.

On March 28, 1950 Audrey recorded "My Tightwad Daddy," "Model T Love," "Help Me Understand" (as a duet with disc jockey Hugh Cherry) and "How Can You Refuse Him Now." On April 4, she recorded "What Put the Pep in Grandma," "I Like That Kind" and "Honky Tonkin'."

During 1950, Hank recorded guitar/vocal demos—probably at Acuff-Rose--of songs he wrote. Those songs were "Message to My Mother," "How Can You Refuse Him Now?," "Last Night I Dreamed of Heaven," "Wearin' Out Your Walkin' Shoes," "There's Nothing As Sweet as My Baby," "'Neath a Cold Gray Tomb of Stone," "I'm Going Home" and "(I'm Gonna) Sing, Sing, Sing."

"Alabama Waltz," was recorded by Bill Monroe on February 3, 1950 and in late 1950 Hank recorded a demo of "Help Me Understand," probably before his Luke the Drifter session.

On June 5, 1950, Curley Williams recorded "Honey Do You Love Me, Huh?," a song he and Hank had written.

CHAPTER

27

Braxton *Shuffert* was an old friend of Hank's from his Montgomery days who used to perform with Hank. Shuffert was working for a meat packing plant when Hank invited him to Nashville and the Grand Ole Opry. Hank wanted to get Braxton back into the music business so he invited Fred Rose over to listen and sign him to MGM.

Hank had written "A Teardrop On a Rose," which Shuffert wanted to record in addition to a non-Acuff-Rose song. Fred Rose did not want him to record a song that Acuff-Rose didn't publish so he encouraged Shuffert and Hank to write an original for the session. Hank and Shuffert wrote "Rockin' Chair Daddy" and, according to Shuffert, "he'd write a line and I'd write a line."

On February 8, 1950 Braxton Shufford recorded "Rockin' Chair Daddy." On October 7 paperwork was filed with the Library of Congress for "Never Been So Lonesome," which had been recorded by Zeb Turner, and "A Teardrop On a Rose."

CHAPTER

28

During a session at the Castle Studio on June 14, 1950, that only lasted an hour and a half (12 noon to 1:30 p.m.) Hank recorded "They'll Never Take Her Love From Me," written by Leon Payne, and "Honky Tonk Blues," which was not issued. Hank had recorded a vocal/guitar demo of "They'll Never Take Her Love From Me" earlier.

"They'll Never Take Her Love From Me" was released on August 18, 1950, entered the *Billboard* country chart on October 7 and reached number five; the "B" side, "Why Should We Try Any More" entered the chart a week later and rose to number nine. This was Hank's twenty-fourth single and his sixteenth and seventeenth chart singles.

CHAPTER

29

Hank recorded four songs between two and five in the afternoon of August 31, 1950 at the Castle studio. The first two songs he recorded, "Nobody's Lonesome For Me" and "Moanin' the Blues" were released as "Hank Williams" while "No, No Joe" and "Help Me Understand" were released as Luke the Drifter.

On this session Hank was backed by his Drifting Cowboy band, Jerry Rivers, Don Helms, Sammy Pruett and Howard Watts ("Cedric Rainwater") (although it is possible that Ernie Newton played bass) with Jack Shook on rhythm guitar. Watts was a popular bass player who served as the comedy man in the band. He replaced Hillous Butram when Butram left the Drifting Cowboys. WSM announcer Farris Coursey played drums—a straight forward drum with brushes and no fills--on "Moanin' the Blues."

"Moanin' the Blues" was released on October 27 with "Nobody's Lonesome For Me" on the "B" side. Both songs entered the *Billboard* country chart on November 18, 1950 and "Moanin' the Blues" became Hank's fourth number one single, staying on the chart for 15 weeks while "Nobody's Lonesome For Me" reached number nine on the chart.

"No, No Joe" was written by Fred Rose about Soviet dictator Joseph Stalin. It was Hank's twenty-fifth single and his third "Luke the Drifter" single. The "B" side was "Help Me Understand."

Although Hank played his guitar on his sessions, it was not miked; Jack Shook played the driving rhythm on this and other Hank Williams sessions.

Tex Ritter recorded "Wearin' Out Your Walkin' Shoes" on September 20, 1950. Charlie Monroe recorded "Sing, Sing, Sing" on October 20, 1950.

In December, 1950 Hank went into the WSM Studio for a March of Dimes broadcast and recorded "Lovesick Blues," "Moanin' The Blues," "(There's a) Bluebird On Your Windowsill" (sung by Audrey), "Help Me Understand" (a duet with Audrey), "When God Dips His Love In My Heart" (written by Cleavant Derricks) and then a reprise of "Lovesick Blues."

He was backed by the Drifting Cowboys, Jerry Rivers, Don Helms and Sammy Pruett with Jack Shook adding rhythm guitar.

CHAPTER

30

Hank recorded "Cold, Cold Heart," "Dear John," "Just Waitin'," and "Men With Broken Hearts" at the Castle Studio on December 21, 1950. Musicians on the session were Drifting Cowboys Jerry Rivers, Don Helms and Sammy Pruett (who played rhythm guitar) with Chet Atkins on electric guitar and either Howard Watts or Ernie Newton on bass and either Owen Bradley or Fred Rose on piano.

The idea for "Cold, Cold Heart" came to Hank after Audrey had an abortion—without his knowledge—and then had to enter the hospital because of an infection. When Hank visited Audrey in the hospital with gifts, she threw them at him; when he returned home, he told the governess who took care of Hank Jr. that Audrey "had a cold cold heart."

The song was released on February 2, 1951 and entered the country chart on March 17. It became Hank's fifth number one single and stayed on the chart for almost a year—46 weeks—with "Dear John," written by Aubrey Gass, on the "B" side. "Dear John" entered the chart two weeks before "Cold, Cold Heart" and reached number eight.

The melody to "Cold, Cold Heart" came from a song, "You'll Still Be In My Heart" written by Ted West in 1943, then re-written by Buddy Starcher. It had been recorded by T. Texas Tyler in

1945. This led to a lawsuit against Hank and Acuff-Rose by Dixie Music and its owner, Clark Van Ness. The suit was not resolved until 1955.

"Just Waitin'," written by Hank and Bob Gazzaway with "Men With Broken Hearts" on the "B" side was released on March 16 as a "Luke the Drifter" single.

During 1951 Hank recorded vocal/guitar demos of "Fool About You" (written by Ralph Hutcheson), "The Angel of Death, "When the Book of Life is Read," "I Can't Escape From You," "Weary Blues From Waitin'," "Ready to Go Home," "California Zephyr" and "Thy Burden's Are Greater Than Mine" (written by Pee Wee King and Redd Stewart).

On January 30, 1951, Carl Smith recorded "There's Nothing As Sweet As My Baby."

CHAPTER

31

cuff-Rose had success on the pop charts with "Tennessee Waltz" by Patti Page and "Chattanoogie Shoeshine Boy" by Red Foley, which encouraged Fred and Wesley Rose to pitch Acuff-Rose songs—including Hank's--to pop artists. Early in 1951 Wesley Rose went to New York with "Cold, Cold Heart," "I Love You Because" by Leon Payne and "Bonaparte's Retreat" by Pee Wee King and Redd Stewart. Tony Bennett recorded "Cold, Cold Heart" on May 31, 1951. The song had been brought to producer Mitch Miller's attention by Jerry Wexler who, at that time, was a journalist with *Billboard*. Bennett was reluctant to record a "country" song but Miller insisted. Bennett had a number one hit with "Because of You" in the summer of 1951; it remained number one for ten weeks. "Cold, Cold Heart" entered the *Billboard* pop chart on July 28 and became Bennett's second number one, remaining in that position for six consecutive weeks.

RCA artists Perry Como and the Fontane Sisters also recorded "Cold, Cold Heart" (Como's did not chart but the Fontane Sisters' version reached number 16). Decca artists Louis Armstrong and Eileen Wilson recorded "Cold, Cold Heart" (Armstrong's version did not chart but Wilson's reached number 19 on the pop chart); and Tony Fontane and Dinah Washington recorded the song for

Mercury (Washington's version did not chart but Fontane's reached number 28).

Because of the success of "Cold, Cold Heart," as well as "Tennessee Waltz" and "Chattanoogie Shoeshine Boy," Columbia producer Mitch Miller reached an agreement with Acuff-Rose for the publisher to send any demos of songs with pop potential to him with the agreement that if Miller recorded a song on a pop artist, that record would not be released until the original version was on the country chart. During the coming years, Acuff-Rose sent a number of songs to Mitch Miller and Nashville acquired a reputation as a "song town," where hit pop songs, as well as country songs, could be found.

CHAPTER

32

On March 16, 1951 Hank was in the studio with Drifting Cowboys Jerry Rivers, Don Helms, Sammy Pruett and Nashville musicians Jerry Shook on rhythm guitar, Ernie Newton or Howard Watts on bass and either Owen Bradley or Fred Rose on piano. They recorded four songs: "I Can't Help It (If I'm Still in Love With You)," "Howlin' At the Moon," "Hey, Good Lookin'," and "My Heart Would Know."

According to Little Jimmy Dickens, Hank wrote "Howlin' at the Moon" and "Hey, Good Lookin'" when they were on a plane headed for an engagement in Wichita Falls, Texas. Hank had a reputation of playing his songs for other country artists and getting their reaction. If the other singers wanted to record the song, Hank might renege and say he was going to record it himself. He had reportedly promised "Hey, Good Lookin'" to Dickens before he reneged on that promise and recorded it himself.

Hank would "get right up close to you in your face," remembered Chet Atkins, "and he'd sing. If you raved over it, he'd love that. He was pitching songs to the hot acts of that time and they'd say 'That's a great song, Hank. I want to do that on my next session.' If he got enough people to say that, he'd say, 'No, it's too damn good for you. I'm gonna do it myself.'" That attitude alienated a number of artists who disliked promises made and then not kept.

Hank apparently wrote "I Can't Help It (If I'm Still in Love With You)" in the car with his band, traveling to an engagement. He came up with the first line, "Today I passed you on the street" and then asked the band members, "What's a good line?" Don Helms deadpanned, "And I smelled your rotten feet." The band members laughed but Hank kept writing.

The hound dog yodels on "Howlin' At the Moon" were supplied by fiddle player Jerry Rivers.

On April 21, the first single from the session was released, "Howlin' At the Moon" with "I Can't Help It (If I'm Still in Love With You)" on the "B" side. The record was a two-sided hit; "Howlin' At the Moon" entered the chart first, on May 26 and reached number three while "I Can't Help It (If I'm Still in Love With You)" entered the chart two weeks later and reached number two. It was Hank's thirtieth single release.

That single was the perfect set-up for Hank's next release, "Hey, Good Lookin'" backed with "My Heart Would Know" on the "B" side.

The single was released on a 78 rpm on June 22, 1951 with "My Heart Would Know" on the "B" side; it entered the *Billboard* country chart on July 14 and rose to number one, where it remained for eight consecutive weeks, and stayed on the chart for 25 weeks; it was his twenty-fourth chart record.

"My Heart Would Know" never charted but earned the same amount of money from record sales as "Hey, Good Lookin'" because it was on the flip side of a hit. That was known in the industry as a "free ride."

"Hey, Good Lookin'" was recorded as a duet by Frankie Laine and Jo Stafford and reached number ten on the pop chart. Guy Mitchell's version of "I Can't Help It" reached number 28 on the pop chart.

CHAPTER

33

Hank and Audrey recorded "The Pale Horse and His Rider" and "Home in Heaven" as a duet on their MGM session on March 23, 1951 backed by Drifting Cowboys Rivers, Helms and Pruett, with Jack Shook on rhythm and Ernie Newton or Howard Watts on bass. "The Pale Horse and His Rider" was written by Ervin Staggs, Johnnie Bailes, Zeke Clements and M.D. Wright. "Home in Heaven" dated back to when Hank was in Montgomery and was on some of the earliest demos Hank sent to Fred Rose.

The record was not released while Hank was alive; it was first released in 1956 on 78 and 45.

CHAPTER

34

During 1951 Hank Williams had a 15-minute radio show on WSM, "Mother's Best," sponsored by "Mother's Best Self-Rising Corn Meal." These shows were recorded at WSM and, after an introduction, Hank generally sang the opening number, then the Drifting Cowboys played a song (usually an instrumental), followed by a gospel song by Hank and then the closing. There were a number of shows where Audrey Williams sang a number alone or as a duet with Hank.

The shows feature Hank singing a number of songs he did not write or record for commercial release. Those songs, many of them gospel songs, include "Where the Old Red River Flows" (Jimmie Davis), "Lord, Build Me a Cabin in Glory" (C.L. Stewart), "Gathering Flowers for the Master's Bouquet" (M. Baumgardner), "The Blind Child's Prayer" (L. Mercer), "Seaman's Blues" (E. Tubb and T. Tubb), "Blue Eyes Crying in the Rain" (Fred Rose), "Wait For the Light to Shine" (Fred Rose), "Pins and Needles (In My Heart)" (Floyd Jenkins/Fred Rose), "Cool Water" (Bob Nolan), "Lonely Tombs" (J. Ellis), "Where the Soul Never Dies" (W. Golden), "Faded Love and Winter Roses" (Fred Rose), "At the First Fall of Snow" (L. Rose), "I'll Fly Away" (Albert Brumley), "Farther Along" (W.B. Stevens-J. Baxter), "Next Sunday, Darling, Is My Birthday" (S. Nathan-A. Smith), "Deck of Cards" (T. Texas Tyler), "When the Fire Comes Down" (Milton Estes-Wally Fowler-T. Harrell-P. Kinsey), "Just When I Needed You" (C. Baum-Jack Anglin-Johnnie Wright), "The Old Country Church" (J. Vaughan), "I Heard My Savior Calling Me" (J. Bailes-Z. Clements-M.D. Wright), "Thirty Pieces of Silver" (O. McLeod), "On Top of Old Smokey" (Public Domain), "I Hang My Head and Cry" (Fred Rose-Ray Whitley-Gene Autry), "At the Cross" (I. Watts-R.E. Hudson), "Low and Lonely" (Floyd Jenkins/Fred Rose), "You Blotted My Happy Schooldays" (L. Fields-I. Messer), "Dust on the Bible" (J. Bailes-W. Bailes-Z. Clements-M.D. Wright), "I've Got My One-Way Ticket to the Sky" (J. Bailes-W. Bailes) and "Searching for a Soldier's Grave" (Roy Acuff).

Songs written by Hank that he performed on the show include "How Can You Refuse Him Now," "Alabama Waltz," "Nobody's Lonesome For Me," "A Mansion on the Hill," "Everything's Okay," "May You Never Be Alone," "Dear Brother," "(Last Night) I Heard You Crying in Your Sleep," "I Just Don't Like This Kind of Livin,'" "On the Banks of the Pontchartrain," "Calling You," "My Sweet Love Ain't Around," "Mind Your Own Business," "Cold, Cold Heart," "I Saw the Light," "Why Don't You Love Me," "Why Should We Try Any More," "Jesus Died for Me," "Long Gone Lonesome Blues," "Moanin' the Blues," "I Can't Help It (If I'm Still in Love With You)," "I'm Gonna Sing," "Just Waitin,'" "I'm So Lonesome I Could Cry," "If I Didn't Love You," "I've Been Down That Road Before" and "Hey, Good Lookin'".

CHAPTER
35

Hank was on the road for most of 1951 and he put together a top notch show. Bill Lister was hired as his warm-up act to open the show, backed by the Drifting Cowboys, then the bass player, Howard Watts, performed comedy as "Cedric Rainwater" and the Drifting Cowboys played a few numbers before Hank took the stage to finish the first half of the show. During intermission the Drifting Cowboys sold song books and photos, then Hank came back and finished the show. In Nashville, Lister appeared on Hank's radio show, "Mother's Best."

On April 24, Big Bill Lister recorded "The Little House We Built Just O'er The Hill," written by Hank and his steel guitar player, Don Helms, and Hank's "Countryfied" for Capitol Records.

Hank's drinking increased and on May 21, he entered a sanatorium in Shreveport. Hank's back bothered him and he was fitted with a brace, but the pain was intense and continuous. He sobered up in Shreveport and made it back to Nashville for a "Luke the Drifter" session.

CHAPTER
36

"Ramblin' Man" was the first song recorded during a session on the evening of June 1, 1951. The other songs recorded on that session were "Picture From Life's Other Side," "I've Been Down That Road Before" and "I Dreamed About Mama Last Night." Musicians on the session were Jerry Rivers, Don Helms, Sammy Pruett, Harold Bradley (rhythm guitar), Ernie Newton or Howard Watts, and possibly Owen Bradley on organ.

The "Luke the Drifter" releases were spoken word songs, but Hank sang "Ramblin' Man." It was released on December 7, 1951 with "Pictures From Life's Other Side" on the "B" side. It was Hank's thirty-fifth single. "Ramblin' Man" was released again, on April 24, 1953, as the "B" side of "Take These Chains From My Heart."

"A Picture From Life's Other Side" was written around 1880 by a singing school teacher, John B. Vaughan from Athens, Georgia. The song had been recorded by J. Frank Smith, Vernon Dalhart and Bradley Kincaid.

Hank's "I've Been Down That Road Before" was released on July 20, 1951 as an "A" side with "I Dreamed About Mama Last Night," which was written by Fred Rose. That single was issued on both 78 and 45 rpm records but never charted. It was released after Hank's hits "Howlin' At the Moon," "I Can't Help It (If I'm Still in Love With You)" and "Hey, Good Lookin'."

On May 6, Charlie Monroe recorded "Jesus Is Calling," a song he wrote with Hank. Hank had recorded a vocal/guitar demo of the song earlier. Carl Smith recorded "Me and My Broken Heart" on June 8, 1951.

During the summer of 1951, Hank recorded a vocal/guitar demo of "Ten Little Numbers," written by Juanita Acuff.

CHAPTER

37

"The Hank Williams Homecoming" was held in Montgomery on Sunday, July 15, and there were two shows that day with Hank Snow, Chet Atkins, The Carter Family and Braxton Schuffert on the program.

Hank had extended his contract with MGM that summer so ten days after the "Homecoming" he was back in the studio recording.

Hank recorded four songs at the Castle Studio on the evening of July 25, 1951, "I'd Still Want You," "(I Heard That) Lonesome Whistle," "Crazy Heart" and "Baby, We're Really in Love." "Crazy Heart" was written by Fred Rose and Maurice Murray and "(I Heard That) Lonesome Whistle" was written by Hank with Jimmie Davis, who claimed to have given Hank the title. Davis, who is credited with co-writing "You Are My Sunshine," had been a local official in Shreveport, where he probably met Hank, and then became Governor of Alabama 1944-1946, campaigning his way into the Governor's office by singing "You Are My Sunshine" at political rallies after telling crowds they had heard enough speeches by the other candidates so he was going to sing 'em a tune. It worked.

Backing Hank were Drifting Cowboys Jerry Rivers, Don Helms and Sammy Pruett; Eddie Hill was probably playing rhythm guitar and either Ernie Newton or Howard Watt was playing bass.

"(I Heard That) Lonesome Whistle" was released on September 14, 1951 with "Crazy Heart" on the "B" side; both songs entered the country chart on October 20 with "Crazy Heart" reaching number four while "Lonesome Whistle" reached number nine.

This version of "I'd Still Want You" was released on November 23, 1951 as the "B" side of a later recording of "Baby, We're Really In Love." The version of "Baby, We're Really in Love" recorded on this session was not issued—it didn't come off well during the session--but Fred Rose liked the song and wanted Hank to record it again.

CHAPTER

38

Hank's next session came just before he left for a ten week tour with the Hadacol Caravan. Fred wanted to have songs ready for release during the time Hank was on tour.

Hank's session at Castle Studio on August 10, 1951 began with him recording a Luke the Drifter song, "I'm Sorry For You My Friend," which was not issued, then "Half as Much," credited to Curley Williams, and second versions of "I'd Still Want You" and "Baby, We're Really in Love." Musicians on the session were Jerry Rivers (fiddle), Don Helms (steel guitar), Sammy Pruett (electric guitar), probably Jack Shook on rhythm guitar and either Ernie Newton or Howard Watts on bass. Possibly Owen Bradley or Marvin Hughes played piano.

"I'm Sorry For You, My Friend" was reportedly written after hearing Lefty Frizzell tell Hank about troubles he had with his wife. "All Hank thought about was writing," remembered Frizzell.

"Half As Much" was written by Curley Williams and Fred Rose insisted that Hank record it; it fit Hank's style perfectly. On "Half As Much" either Fred or Owen Bradley played piano. Curley Williams recorded the song for Columbia on September 13 and his version was released in November. Rosemary Clooney covered the song and it became her second number one (her first was "Come On-A My House") the following year.

This session's recording of "Baby, We're Really in Love" was the "A" side of his thirty-fourth single, released on November 23,

1951; the "B" side was the first version of "I'd Still Want You." ("The second version of "I'd Still Want You" was not released until 1984 when it was on an album, *Rare Takes and Radio Cuts*.)

The single of "Baby, We're Really In Love" was issued on both 78 and 45 rpm formats and was released in England in 1952. It entered the *Billboard* Country chart on December 22, 1951 and reached number four in 1952, remaining there for 15 weeks. The "B" side, "I'd Still Want You," did not chart. This was Hank's twenty-seventh chart record.

"Half as Much" was released on March 28, 1952, seven months after it was recorded, with "Let's Turn Back the Years" on the "B" side. It followed "Lonesome Whistle" and "Crazy Heart" and did not enter the *Billboard* country chart until December 21, then rose to number four and remained on the chart for 15 weeks.

There are vocal/guitar recordings by Hank made on September 15, 1951. The songs were "Half As Much," "Lovesick Blues," "(I Heard that) Lonesome Whistle," "Honky Tonk Blues" and "Where the Old Red River Flows."

Hank had a number of his songs recorded by other artists, but none were big hits. Little Jimmy Dickens recorded "I Wish You Didn't Love Me So Much" on July 12, 1951. It was later re-written and recorded by Hank as "Why Don't You Make Up Your Mind." On October 14, 1951, Jimmie Davis recorded two songs he and Hank had written, "Bayou Pon Pon" and "Forever Is a Long Time." Rusty Gabbard and Ray Price both recorded "I Can't Escape From You." "A Stranger In the Night," written by Hank and Bill Morgan, brother of Opry star George Morgan (whose big hits were "Candy Kisses" and "Room Full of Roses") was recorded by George Morgan.

CHAPTER

39

"Big Bill" Lister (he stood six foot seven) needed a beer drinking song and asked Hank if he had one; Hank told him he would write one. "Beer Drinkin' Blues" had been a jukebox hit for Lister and he needed a follow-up because drinking songs were popular on jukeboxes, although they received no radio airplay. Lister's session for Capitol was scheduled for October 26 and the night before the session Hank recorded a vocal/guitar demo of "There's a Tear in My Beer" and another song, "All the Love I Ever Had" with just his guitar.

"There's a Tear in My Beer" has an interesting history that went from being a "lost" demo to a Grammy winning song 38 years later.

After Lister's session, he tossed the acetate into a box of records he had at home. At the end of the year, Lister decided to move back to San Antonio and give up his music career. The cardboard box of records sat outside Lister's house, covered by a tarp, for several years, then was moved to the attic where it endured heat and cold until the mid-1980s when Lister found the unmarked demo while cleaning his house. Hank Williams Jr. is a gun enthusiast and Lister's son had done gun work for Hank Jr., repairing guns in his collection. During an appearance by Hank, Jr. in San Antonio, Lister gave him the demo, saying "This is one they ain't never heard your Daddy do."

Hank Jr. knew he had a treasure and was determined to record a duet with his father on the song, accompanied by a video of Hank performing "Hey, Good Lookin'" on "The Kate Smith Evening Hour." In September, 1988, Hank Jr. recorded the song as a duet. The video of Hank Senior was doctored to make it appear he was singing "There's a Tear in My Beer." The duet entered the *Billboard* country chart on February 4, 1989 and won a Grammy for "Best Vocal Country Collaboration," beating out the duet of Ringo Starr and Buck Owens doing "Act Naturally," a song the Beatles recorded with Ringo singing lead back in 1965.

The vocal/acoustic demos of both "There's a Tear In My Beer" and "All the Love I Ever Had" were not released until 1998 on *The Complete Hank Williams* boxed set.

On September 15, 1951, Hank recorded a guitar/vocal demo of "Honky Tonk Blues."

CHAPTER

40

The final days of the Hadacol empire created by Dudley Joseph LeBlanc came to an end on September 17, 1951. The Hadacol Caravan, featuring Hank and Minnie Pearl, was scheduled to run from August 14 to October 2 but on September 17 it all fell apart with bounced checks and debt. The following year, LeBlanc declared bankruptcy.

On October 16, Ray Price recorded "Weary Blues From Waitin'" for Columbia. Price, a new artist, befriended Hank and during a road trip Hank told him "you need a hit" and wrote "Weary Blues From Waitin'" in the car as they drove. Price claimed that he took part in the writing but his name is not on the song.

Hank had important national television appearances during the Fall of 1951. On October 11 he was on "The Kate Smith Evening Hour" and on November 14, he sang "Hey, Good Lookin'" on Perry Como's Show on CBS.

CHAPTER
41

ountry music was not an album-oriented genre during the 1950s. The 12 inch long–playing record was developed by Columbia, primarily for Broadway cast recordings. Top artists concentrated on singles and in country music, most of those singles were bought by jukeboxes, which were the financial foundation for country music. Albums were mostly shunned by country music executives, including Fred Rose, who felt it took the focus off singles, which were their bread and butter.

Hank's first album, Hank Williams Sings, was released on November 9, 1952. It contained eight songs, "House Without Love," "Wedding Bells," "Mansion on the Hill," "Wealth Won't Save Your Soul," "I Saw the Light," "Six More Miles," "Lost Highway" and "I've Just Told Mama Good-Bye."

On October 30, 1951, Rusty Gabbard recorded "I Can't Escape From You."

CHAPTER

42

Hank's third recording of "Honky Tonk Blues" with a full band occurred on December 11, 1951 at the Castle Studio. Backed by Jerry Rivers, Don Helms, Sammy Pruett, probably Jack Shook, rhythm guitar and Ernie Newton or Howard Watts on bass, the session lasted two hours, from 10 a.m. until noon.

"Honky Tonk Blues" was the second song recorded, after "I'm Sorry For You, My Friend" and before "Let's Turn Back the Years." Both "Honky Tonk Blues" and "Let's Turn Back the Years" dated back to his Montgomery days, although "Honky Tonk Blues" had been re-written and some original lines had been dropped.

This is the last session where Hank recorded with all of his band members.

"Honky Tonk Blues" was released on February 2, 1952 with "I'm Sorry For You My Friend," a Luke the Drifter song, on the "B" side. "Honky Tonk Blues" entered the country chart on March 1, 1952 and rose to number two, remaining on the chart for 12 weeks. It followed "Baby, We're Really in Love." "I'm Sorry For You, My Friend" did not chart.

"Let's Turn Back the Years" was the "B" side of "Half as Much," which was released in March, 1952.

By the end of 1951 Hank was exhausted and in constant pain. He was on the road constantly, his back hurt, the price of fame was bearing down and he was drinking more frequently. The court case by Dixie Music against Acuff-Rose caused Hank's publisher to freeze income from "Cold, Cold Heart." The money was held in escrow until 1955 when Dixie Music was awarded $5,000. By that time, there was $42,000 in the escrow account.

CHAPTER

43

O n January 14, 1952 "When The Book of Life Is Read" was recorded by Jimmie Skinner. On February 8, 1952 Ray Price recorded "I Lost the Only Love I Knew," written by Hank and Don Helms. "My Cold, Cold Heart is Melted Now" (written by Hank and Johnnie Masters) was probably written about the same time but was not recorded by Kitty Wells until July 10, 1953.

In April, 1952 Hank recorded vocal/guitar demos of "Are You Walkin' And a Talkin' For the Lord" and three songs he didn't write, "Wild Side of Life" (a hit for Hank Thompson written by Arlie A. Carter-William Warren), "I Cried Again" (Autry Inman) and "Drifting Too Far From the Shore" (Charles E. Moody).

The spring of 1952 was a turbulent one for Hank. On March 5 he took the Drifting Cowboys off his payroll; in April the divorce terms with Audrey were settled and Hank had a new girlfriend, Bobbie Jett.

CHAPTER

44

"Jambalaya (On the Bayou)" was first recorded as a guitar/vocal demo before it was recorded with a full band on June 13, 1952 in a session at the Castle Studio that began at 10 a.m. and ran until 1 p.m. Hank's guitar player, Sammy Pruett, had joined Carl Smith's band, the Tunesmiths, so Chet Atkins played electric guitar on this song, joined by Drifting Cowboys Jerry Rivers and Don Helms with Jack Shook on rhythm guitar and Willis Brothers member Charles "Indian" Wright on bass.

The first song on the session, "Window Shopping," was by New York journalist Marcel Joseph. "Jambalaya" was the second song on the session, followed by "Settin' The Woods On Fire," written by Fred Rose and Ed Nelson, and "I'll Never Get Out of This World Alive," credited to Hank and Fred Rose.

Hank's name appears alone on "Jambalaya" but it was co-written with Cajun pianist Moon Mullican, known as "King of the Hillbilly Piano Players." Moon (whose real name was Aubrey Wilson Mullican), had been in Jimmie Davis' band at KWKH in Shreveport and formed his own band in 1945. He had a hit with "New Pretty Blonde," a nonsense version of the Cajun hit "Jole Blon." Hank brought him to the Grand Ole Opry in 1951 and they wrote "Jambalaya," which owed a great deal to the Cajun hit, "Big Texas" by Papa Cairo. It also owed a great deal to "Gran' Texas" by Chuck Guillory. Mullican received royalties from "Jambalaya" under the table due to the fact that he was signed to King Records and their publishing company, Louis Music.

"Jambalaya" was released on July 18, 1952, entered the *Billboard* country chart on August 16 and became a huge hit, reaching number one, where it remained for 14 weeks and stayed on the chart for 29 weeks. The "B" side was "Window Shopping."

This was the thirty-eighth single released by Hank and the thirtieth to chart.

MGM released a Luke the Drifter single, "Why Don't You Make Up Your Mind" b/w "Be Careful of Stones That You Throw" before they released "Settin' The Woods on Fire" with "You Win Again" on the "B" side. That single was released on September 22 and "Settin' The Woods on Fire" reached number two while "You Win Again" reached number ten on the *Billboard* chart.

"I'll Never Get Out of This World Alive" (the title came from a phrase popularized by comedian W.C. Fields) was on the *Billboard* country chart at the time of Hank's death on January 1, 1953. Written by Hank with Fred Rose, it had entered the chart on December 20, 1952, less than two weeks before his death, and reached number one on the chart after his death.

The song had been released on November 21, 1952 with "I Could Never Be Ashamed of You" on the "B" side. "I'll Never Get Out of This World Alive" is actually a humorous song with the dark side of Hank's humor showing through. It was the forty-first single released by Hank and his thirty-third chart record.

Chet Atkins remembered, "We recorded 'I'll Never Get Out of This World Alive' [and] after each take, he'd sit down in a chair. I remember thinking, 'Hoss, you're not just jivin' because he was so weak and all he could do was just sing a few lines, and then just fall in the chair."

In line with Acuff-Rose's efforts to obtain pop records with their country songs, MGM president Frank Walker gave Art Mooney and His Orchestra "Window Shopping" (it did not chart) and "Settin' The Woods on Fire" to Fran Warren (it did not chart either) but did not send "Jambalaya" to any of his artists. Columbia head Mitch Miller recorded "Jambalaya" with Jo Stafford (it reached number three on the pop chart) and "Settin' the Woods on Fire" as a duet with Jo Stafford and Frankie Laine (it reached number 21 on the pop chart).

CHAPTER

45

Hank's divorce from Audrey was final by July 11 and on that day Hank was in the Castle Studio with musicians Jerry Rivers, Don Helms, Chet Atkins, Jack Shook and Ernie Newton. The group recorded "You Win Again," "I Won't Be Home No More," "Be Careful of Stones That You Throw" (written by Bonnie Dodd) and "Why Don't You Make Up Your Mind."

The songs sound like they were written for Audrey—and they probably were. Given that the divorce proceedings progressed through the first half of 1952, "You Win Again," "I Won't Be Home No More," "Be Careful of Stones That You Throw" and especially "Why Don't You Make Up Your Mind" are songs about Hank's marriage and life with Audrey.

"You Win Again" was originally titled "I Lose Again" but Fred Rose convinced Hank to change it to "You Win Again." It was on the "B" side of "Settin' The Woods on Fire," released on September 12. A month earlier "You Win Again" was recorded by Tommy Edwards on MGM and the song entered the *Billboard* pop chart on November 29 and reached number 13.

"Be Careful of Stones That You Throw" had been around awhile before Fred Rose found it and pitched it to Hank. It was written by steel guitarist Bonnie Dodd and Little Jimmie Dickens had recorded it. Dickens had also recorded "I Wish You Didn't

Love Me So Much," which Hank re-wrote and re-named "Why Don't You Make Up Your Mind," a bitter, vengeful song.

The day after the session, Hank debuted "Jambalaya" on the Grand Ole Opry and the day after that—July 12--Hank was in West Grove, Pennsylvania at Sunset Park where a local musician, Melvin Price, recorded Hank's show—or at least 30 minutes of it. Backing Hank were Jerry Rivers and Don Helms from the Drifting Cowboys, with Bobby Montgomery on rhythm guitar and Roy Perkins on bass. The songs Hank sang that day were "Hey, Good Lookin,'" "(I Heard That) Lonesome Whistle," "Jambalaya (On the Bayou)," "Long Gone Lonesome Blues," "Half as Much," "I Saw the Light" and "Lovesick Blues." There was a comedy sketch and Jerry Rivers played the fiddle tune, "Fire On The Mountain."

After this session, Hank went on a drinking binge. He had been living on Natchez Trace in Nashville, sharing a house with Ray Price. He ordered Price to leave—and he did—but Price and Don Helms got Hank into a sanitarium in Madison, a Nashville suburb. By this time, Hank had a new girlfriend, Billie Jean Jones. He met her when Faron Young brought her to the Opry. Hank was quickly infatuated and convinced Faron to trade dates with him; Faron didn't argue.

CHAPTER

46

On August 11, 1952, Jim Denny called Hank and told him he was fired from the Opry. It was a crushing blow for Hank but Denny, who booked Hank, felt he had no choice. The drinking and failure to appear for shows—or appear on the shows drunk—was too much for the Opry, which was intent on preserving its image and reputation.

Hank had moved back to Montgomery by this time and lived in his mother's boarding house. He went to a lodge on Kowaliga Bay with Bobbie Jett and some friends and during a car trip, Hank began pounding on the dashboard and singing "Kowaliga, Kowaliga." That evening, Hank worked on the song and the next morning a deejay, Bob McKinnon, who had been with Hank (and bailed him out of jail after Hank was arrested after creating an unpleasant scene at a hotel in Alexander City) called Fred Rose in Nashville. McKinnon passed along the message that Hank wanted Rose to come to Montgomery so they could work on this song.

During his time in the Kowaliga Bay area, Hank also wrote "Your Cheatin' Heart" and "Lonesomest Time of the Day," although Billie Jean stated that Hank had started "Your Cheatin' Heart" in their car driving to Louisiana. Murray Nash, an Acuff-Rose employee, had driven down with Rose and taped Hank singing demos of "Your Cheatin' Heart" and "Lonesomest Time of the

Day." Rose found some time alone and re-wrote "Kowaliga" into "Kaw-Liga" with a minor chord opening and a story line about a wooden Indian.

Rose managed to get Hank back on the "Louisiana Hayride" as a step towards getting him back on the Opry. "Jambalaya (On the Bayou)" was hot and MGM was busy pressing records and sending them to distributors and retailers.

CHAPTER

47

Hank's last professional recording session took place at the familiar Castle Studio on September 23, 1952—six days after his twenty-ninth birthday. Backed by Tommy Jackson on fiddle, Don Helms on steel guitar, Chet Atkins on electric guitar, Eddie Hill on rhythm guitar and Floyd "Lightnin'" Chance on bass, he recorded "I Could Never Be Ashamed of You," "Your Cheatin' Heart," "Kaw-Liga" (credited to Hank and Fred Rose) and "Take These Chains From My Heart" (by Fred Rose and Ty Heath). "I Could Never Be Ashamed of You" was apparently inspired by Billie Jean; Hank told her that, unlike his life with Audrey, he could never be ashamed of her. For "Kaw-Liga," Rose brought in Farris Coursey, a WSM announcer and drummer with the WSM house band.

It was obvious that Hank was having troubles; two previous sessions, on September 9 and September 19 were cancelled after they had been scheduled.

For "Your Cheatin' Heart," Hank borrowed the melody of "Your Cold, Cold Heart is Melted Now," credited to Hank and Johnny Masters, that had been written prior to "Your Cheatin' Heart."

Acuff-Rose lost no time in sending copies of those songs to pop producers. Frank Walker gave "Your Cheatin' Heart" to MGM artist Joni James and her version reached number two on the pop chart the following year, remaining on the chart for 17 weeks. Mitch Miller gave "Your Cheatin' Heart" to Tony Bennett, who was no longer reluctant to record country songs; his version reached number eight on the pop chart the following year. Dolores Gray recorded "Kaw-Liga" for Decca and it reached number 23 on the pop chart.

In October, Hank agreed to provide financial support to Bobbie Jett, who was pregnant with Hank's child. (Jett Williams was born January 6, 1953.) On October 19 he married Billie Jean Jones during a show at the Municipal Auditorium in New Orleans; in fact, he married her twice—at the afternoon show and again during that evening's show.

On November 21 Hank's forty-first single—and the last that was issued during his lifetime--was released. "I'll Never Get Out of This World Alive" became a number one single after his death. The "B" side, "I Could Never Be Ashamed of You" did not chart.

During 1952 Hank had recorded vocal/guitar demos of "Are You Walkin' And A-Talkin' For the Lord," "You Better Keep It On Your Mind," "A Teardrop on a Rose," "I Ain't Got Nothin' But Time," "Low Down Blues" and "If You'll Be a Baby To Me." "Are You Walkin and A-Talkin' For the Lord" was recorded by Wilma Lee and Stony Cooper on February 17, 1953

Hank Williams' last recording was a vocal/guitar demo of "The Log Train" that he recorded in Nashville on December 3, 1952.

CHAPTER
48

Hank Williams had been a chronic drinker since his teens. In *Sing a Sad Song*, Roger Williams writes, "Why did alcohol get a foothold with Hank when it did? His moonshine revelries could not have been responsible, not unless one accepts the theory that persons with an innate craving for alcohol are sure to become alcoholics once they taste it. The hectic, freewheeling life of the honky tonk musician is more to blame; drinking was a natural by-product of that sort of life. But the main reason has to be Hank's basic emotional deficiencies. He was proving himself incapable, even at an early age, of coping with his life and problems in a straightforward fashion. Hank's drinking remained a problem throughout the rest of his life, contributing heavily toward his personal problems, his professional undependability and demise and, ultimately, to his early, untimely death."

On June 11, 1949, Hank Williams was the newest--and greatest--sensation on the Grand Ole Opry. On August 11, 1952, just three years later, Hank Williams was told by Opry manager Jim Denny that he was no longer a member of the Opry. At 28, Hank's career was heading downhill quickly.

After his split from the Opry, Williams moved back to Shreveport where, once again, he joined the Louisiana Hayride. Fred Rose and Jim Denny were both influential in this decision;

apparently they wanted Hank to go back to Shreveport and reestablish himself and put his career and personal life back in line, before they would attempt to bring him back to the Opry. Jim Denny reportedly promised Hank that he would possibly line up an appearance in February, 1953. According to reports, Hank called Denny every day after leaving the Opry to see if he could be reinstated.

The move to Shreveport did not help Hank straighten up. If anything, it made him worse--adding another reason for drink to pad his wounded pride.

CHAPTER

49

Hank and Audrey had separated in January, 1952 with Audrey filing for "separate maintenance." Later, she changed the suit to divorce and it was granted in Nashville. Hank had moved out of the Franklin Road home and into a house on Natchez Trace with singer Ray Price. Hank lost property and earnings in the divorce as well as custody of his son, Randall Hank.

Audrey was granted half of all songwriting and record royalties that Hank would generate in the future, a settlement that left her comfortable for life. But though Hank gave up property and income, he never quite gave up his feelings and remained in love with her the rest of his life. Still, he tried marriage on the rebound, marrying Billie Jean Jones, nineteen year old daughter of the Bossier City, Louisiana, police chief during a show in New Orleans. He admitted later he had married the young, pretty Billie Jean "to spite Audrey."

During this time Hank's health was declining rapidly. He was hopelessly addicted to alcohol and pills. He didn't--perhaps couldn't--sleep or rest and was therefore constantly fatigued. Sometime during that fall in Shreveport Hank began seeing a man named Toby Marshall, a quack doctor who supplied Hank with amphetamines, Seconal and chloral hydrate, a sedative that apparently helped ease the constant physical pain his back gave him.

CHAPTER

50

Hank was booked on a New Year's Eve show in Charleston, West Virginia and for a show in Canton, Ohio on January 1, 1953, his first show dates out of the deep south since his release from the Opry. It was important that he appear sober and do well on these dates. Hank called Don Helms of the Drifting Cowboys band to see if the band could back him on the Canton date. The Drifting Cowboys, who had ceased depending on Hank for work except for an occasional date, were booked to perform with Ray Price on that day in nearby Cleveland. Helms reached an agreement with Hank that the band would spilt to back both acts so that Helms backed Williams and Jerry Rivers backed Ray Price.

Hank left Montgomery on December 30 for Charleston but only made it to Birmingham because of a snow storm. The next day he continued on, getting to Knoxville, where he booked a flight to Charleston; however, the plane had to return to Knoxville and Hank had to drive from there to Canton. For the trip he had hired an eighteen year old Montgomery cab driver to drive while he slept and rested in the back seat of his Cadillac. With him in the back seat was a bottle of whisky and some chloral hydrate from "Dr." Marshall.

In Knoxville, Hank visited a physician and received a shot, apparently to ease the pain in his back. About an hour outside Knoxville, near Rutledge, Tennessee, the Cadillac was stopped by a state trooper and the driver given a ticket for speeding. As he was giving the ticket, the trooper noticed Hank in the back seat and remarked "That guy looks dead." The driver, Charles Carr, replied that he had taken a sedative and was sleeping, then went on his way.

As Carr drove for the next five hours, he grew increasingly concerned about Hank but, not wanting to risk his ire at being awakened, did not stop until he arrive in Oak Hill, West Virginia where he pulled into a service station. When Carr reached back to check on him he touched Hank's cold hand. Carr drove quickly to the Oak Hill Hospital where Hank Williams was pronounced dead. The cause listed was a heart attack. He was 29 years old.

In Canton, Ohio the news of Hank's death was announced to the crowded audience at the auditorium by local disc jockey Cliff Rogers, who was serving as master of ceremony for the show. He announced that before the show began there would be a small tribute to Hank. The room was darkened and a single spotlight shone on the empty stage as the cast, which included Hawkshaw Hawkins, Homer and Jethro, Kitty Wells, Johnnie and Jack, June Webb and the Drifting Cowboys sang "I Saw The Light" from behind the closed curtain.

CHAPTER

51

None of the songs recorded during his last session in September were released during Hank's lifetime, but in the year following his death they dominated the country chart in *Billboard*.

On January 30—a month after Hank's death—MGM released a two sided hit, "Your Cheatin' Heart" and "Kaw-Liga." Both songs entered the chart on February 21 and both rose to number one. "Kaw Liga" remained in the number one slot for 13 weeks while "Your Cheatin' Heart" held the number one spot for six weeks.

"Take These Chains From My Heart," with "Ramblin Man" on the "B" side, was released on May 16 and rose to number one and held that spot for four straight weeks.

Hank Williams was the hottest act in country music at the time of his death and Fred Rose needed more releases from Hank. MGM released an album, *Hank Williams Memorial*, that contained "Cold, Cold Heart," "Your Cheatin' Heart," "Settin' The Woods On Fire," "Kaw-Liga," "You Win Again," "I Could Never Be Ashamed of You," "Hey, Good Lookin'" and "Half as Much" in 1953. The label also released an album, *Hank Williams as Luke The Drifter* that contained "Picture From Life's Other Side," "Help Me Understand," "Be Careful of Stones That You Throw," "Funeral," "Please Make Up Your Mind," "Just Waitin,"

"Men With Broken Hearts," "Too Many Parties, Too Many Pals," "I Dreamed About Mama Last Night," "Beyond the Sunset," "I've Been Down That Road Before" and "Everything's O.K."

CHAPTER

52

During the year after Hank's death, Fred Rose took some of Hank's guitar/vocal demos into the studio for musicians to add full instrumentation. On July 8, 1953, with Chet Atkins and Sammy Pruett on guitar, Don Helms on steel, and Chuck "Indian" Wright on bass, Rose supervised the backing on three songs written by Hank, "Weary Blues From Waitin,'" "I Can't Escape From You" and "You Better Keep It On Your Mind."

The next day, fiddler Jerry Rivers joined the group for a long session where they overdubbed seven songs: "A Teardrop On a Rose," "How Can You Refuse Him Now?," "The Angel of Death," "I Ain't Got Nothin' But Time," "A House of Gold," "We're Getting Closer to the Grave Each Day" and "Low Down Blues."

MGM released "I Won't Be Home No More" backed with "My Love For You (Has Turned to Hate)" in July, 1953. "I Won't Be Home No More" reached number four on the country chart. In September, the label released the overdubbed demos of "Weary Blues From Waitin'" and "I Can't Escape From You." "Weary Blues From Waitin'" entered the *Billboard* chart in October but only reached number seven. In November, MGM released two cuts from the Sterling sessions, "Calling You" and "When God Comes and Gathers His Jewels." Neither side charted.

Rose continued to overdub a backing band on Hank's demos;
on September 24, 1954, the Drifting Cowboys provided overdubs
on five of Hank's songs: "(I'm Gonna) Sing, Sing, Sing," "California
Zephyr," "Message To My Mother," "Mother Is Gone" and "Ready
To Go Home."

On December 1, 1954, Fred Rose died; his son, Wesley,
would now be the one to promote the Hank Williams catalog and
nurture his legacy. It was the end of an era; although Hank's demos
continued to be overdubbed, the team of Hank Williams and Fred
Rose, who were the heart and soul of Hank's songs and recordings,
was gone.

After the death of Hank Williams, the legend was born, a
legend that continues as new fans learn of Hank and his timeless
songs and untimely death.

CHAPTER

53

The Acuff-Rose offices on Franklin Road in Nashville had a hidden treasure. In Hank's book that he wrote on songwriting he stated that a songwriter should keep a notebook of songs, along with ideas. Hank practiced what he preached.

Hank carried a brown leather briefcase with him and in that briefcase he had a notebook(s) as well as ideas and scraps of songs. At the time of his death, he had four notebooks of songs with the lyrics hand-written. There was also a cardboard box where Hank tossed song lyrics or bits of songs. The melodies were in Hank's head, because he could neither read nor write music.

After Hank died, his mother, Lillian, contacted Fred Rose about the briefcase, the cardboard box and notebooks. Shortly after Hank died, Fred and Wesley Rose went to Montgomery and took possession of those songs. Acuff-Rose employee Peggy Lamb was the guardian of the treasures; they were kept in a fireproof safe sitting beside her desk.

Wesley Rose made sure the sixty-six lyrics were copyrighted.

The songs in the notebook, written by Hank, usually included the date when he wrote the lyrics into the notebook. During the 1960s, when Hank Williams, Jr. was starting his career, Wesley Rose let him have some of the lyrics to write melodies to. Some of the lyrics were not complete so Hank Jr. completed them. Hank

Jr. recorded those songs on several albums. The songs Hank, Jr. added melodies (and some lyrics) to from those notebooks are "Are You Lonely Too," "Cajun Baby," "For Me This Is No Place," "Homesick," "I'm Just Crying Cause I Care," "I'm So Tired of It All," "Is This Goodbye?," "Just Me and My Broken Heart," "My Heart Won't Let Me Go," "Somebody's Lonesome," "Where Do I Go From Here?," "You Broke Your Own Heart," "You Can't Take My Memories of You" and "Your Turn To Cry."

CHAPTER

54

In October, 1982, the insurance company American General took over the National Life and Insurance Company and sold WSM, the Grand Ole Opry, Opryland Hotel, the Opryland Theme Park and the Ryman Auditorium to Ed Gaylord, who owned the "Hee Haw" television show. Gaylord, based on Oklahoma City, paid $400 million for those assets. In May, 1985, Gaylord purchased Acuff-Rose Publishing.

Acuff-Rose remained on Franklin Road until 1986, when Gaylord built an office building on Music Row at the corner of 17th Avenue South and Grand Avenue and moved the Acuff-Rose operation into that building. Among the treasures they held were the Hank Williams notebooks as well as other key Acuff-Rose documents stored in two large fireproof vaults.

Acuff-Rose publishing was part of the Opryland Music Group, headed by Jerry Bradley and Troy Tomlinson. In 2002, the Opryland Music Group, including Acuff-Rose, was sold to Sony/ATV Publishing.

MGM Records, the label that Hank recorded for, had undergone changes in ownership through the years. In 1972, the MGM label was sold to Polygram; in 1976 it was absorbed into the Polydor label. In 1998, Polygram was sold to the Universal Music Group. The Nashville office of Universal was in charge of the country music catalogue and released records on their Mercury label.

The 1990s saw the music industry explode with the acceptance of the Compact Disc, which had originally been introduced in the United States in 1983. As the music industry evolved from vinyl records to cassette tapes to CDs, consumers purchased their favorite albums and artists on the CD format. Labels packaged catalogues of favorite artists into boxed sets, which sold well in the CD format. This led Mercury Records in Nashville to compile a boxed set of Hank Williams' recordings, including demos of his songs as well as songs recorded for MGM.

Mercury Records executive Kira Florita was in charge of working with the Country Music Hall of Fame to put together a boxed set of Hank's recordings. This is how Florita came to learn about the notebooks at Acuff-Rose.

Florita and Colin Escott co-authored a picture book of Hank Williams' memorabilia, *Snapshots from the Lost Highway*, which was published in 2001. In the book were images of the notebooks with several unrecorded songs.

There was interest in Hank Williams at the end of the 1990s, spurred on by a push from Mercury Records to promote their Hank Williams catalogue. This led to an album, *Timeless*, featuring contemporary artists' interpretations of some of Hank's songs. The album was produced by Mary Martin, Luke Lewis and Bonnie Garner; on the album were Bob Dylan ("I Can't Get You Off Of My Mind"), Sheryl Crow ("Long Gone Lonesome Blues"), Keb' Mo' ("I'm So Lonesome I Could Cry"), Beck ("Your Cheatin' Heart"), Mark Knopfler and His Band ("Lost On The River"), Tom Petty ("You're Gonna Change (Or I'm Gonna Leave"), Keith Richards

("You Win Again"), Emmylou Harris ("Alone and Forsaken"), Hank Williams III ("I'm a Long Gone Daddy"), Ryan Adams ("Lovesick Blues'), Lucinda Williams ("Cold, Cold Heart") and Johnny Cash ("I Dreamed About Mama Last Night").

The *Timeless* album was released in 2001 and won a Grammy.

Mary Martin had learned about the notebooks from Florita's and Escott's book. Then, in 2002, after Sony/ATV had purchased the Acuff-Rose catalogue, a meeting between Sony/ATV head Donna Hilley, Florita, Peggy Lamb and Peggy Martin led to the decision to allow well-known singer/songwriters to write melodies to Hank's lyrics and record them for the Country Music Hall of Fame's boxed set. The agreement was that Sony-ATV, through Acuff-Rose, would control the copyrights; there would be no "split" copyrights with another publishing company because a songwriter had written a melody for the song.

Mary Martin had worked for Albert Grossman during the 1960s when he managed Bob Dylan; Martin approached Dylan about the project and he agreed to participate. Dylan decided to only do one song and allow other artists to fill out the album.

The songs and artists were "You've Been Lonesome, Too" by Alan Jackson, "The Love That Faded" by Bob Dylan, "How Many Times Have You Broken My Heart?" by Norah Jones, "You Know That I Know" by Jack White, "I'm So Happy I Found You" by Lucinda Williams, "I Hope You Shed a Million Tears" by Vince Gill and Rodney Crowell, "You're Through Fooling Me" by Patty Loveless (with Emory Gordy, Jr. as co-writer), "You'll Never Again Be Mine" by Levon Helm (with Larry Campbell as co-writer), "Blue Is My Heart" by Holly Williams, "Mama, Come Home" by Jakob Dylan, "Angel Mine" by Sheryl Crow, and "The Sermon On the Mount" by Merle Haggard.

CHAPTER

55

Hank Williams was more than a songwriter--he was a true poet. He has been called "the hillbilly Shakespeare" and the title is certainly appropriate. Shakespeare reached the masses with his words and, especially his sonnets, evoke a "feel" all their own, verbalizing the feelings we all have. Hank Williams did the same thing.

In America today, there seems to be a shortage of poets-- or at least a shortage in famous American poets. Commercially, they're at the bottom; poetry books sell few copies. There also seems to be a lack of respect for the profession of "poet." The void here is filled by songwriters. Indeed, if you call to mind the poets best acquainted with the American public in recent years you will probably come up with names such as Bob Dylan, Kris Kristofferson, Joni Mitchell, Merle Haggard, Paul Simon and other songwriters. Hank Williams too is a poet. His poems are his songs. As songs, they represent one of the most influential bodies of work ever presented to writers, artists and the public. His influence, not just in country music but other forms as well, is understatedly tremendous. Anyone who has let themselves study and listen to Hank Williams' music is a convert--and almost certainly influenced by him in one form or another. As poems, his songs stand up well, straightforward with raw, earthy feelings expressed in the language of the everyday man.

Hank Williams did not write for highbrows; his lyrics reflect a class of "average" people.

Listening to Hank Williams' songs, three themes become apparent. First is a light-hearted sense of humor, an ability to laugh at himself even in his sadness and despair; second is a strong religious belief, especially in the afterlife; and third is a deep, sad, loneliness.

The humorous songs represent the lighter side of Hank--the funny, fun-loving character that he was. It is ironic to note that, although the image of Hank Williams is wrapped heavily in tragedy and sadness, Wesley Rose, who knew Hank well, remembered him best as a laughing, fun-lover. This is no doubt true--many others who knew Hank have funny stories to tell. However, his partying and humorous antics carry a strong sense of self-destructiveness with them.

To say that Hank Williams was a religious man, meaning that he was pious, would be untrue. Yet this complex man obviously did have a strong, deep belief through which he would draw closer to God. But however great those flashes of light were for Hank, it did not seem to glow constantly for him. His religious songs seem to reflect emotional, heartfelt moments but not a continuing and constant way of life.

The predominant themes in the songs of Hank Williams are hurt, sadness, loneliness and despair. Even in his humorous and religious songs, this sadness is heard and felt. On the whole, Hank's sad songs are his best and most memorable. Even today, people know his songs of sadness. Too, his image of a lonely tortured man show through clearly in these songs. This has aided and embellished that image, and is a fairly accurate reflection of the inner Hank, the heart and soul of the man behind the genius.

CHAPTER

56

enius is part instinctive, part intuitive. The genius cannot explain himself, cannot really say how or why he created what he did. There is the subconscious always at work, developing and springing forth new ideas, new lines, new phrases. The genius cannot say where it all comes from; he sees the river but cannot explain the deep spring feeding it. It is up to others to analyze, define, categorize the work; the true genius is only capable of creating it. Especially a genius such as Hank Williams, who could not really understand or explain his writing--he could only do it.

Hank wrote a book on songwriting with Jimmy Rule which was published by Harpeth Press in 1951. Titled *Hank Williams Tells How to Write Folk and Western Music to Sell*, it is obvious Williams is inarticulate concerning his own songwriting talent. The book is full of obvious, surface advice, such as "Carry a little book with you at all times in which you can jot down any title that you think or hear from other sources" or "It would be difficult to say whether the words or the tune has most to do with the success of a song. It is usually a combination of both good words and a good tune but that certainly is not always true" or this gem, "You should avoid especially the offending of any religious groups or any races. It goes without saying that you must observe all standards of decency. Avoid writing songs that have or could have double meanings or could be interpreted in any indecent manner."

Hank has been quoted as saying his songs "just come bustin' out" which Roger Williams notes is a "colorful but not too informative way of putting it." The creative process of Hank Williams writing a song was perhaps described best by Jerry Rivers, a member of the Drifting Cowboys. In a set of liner notes, Rivers stated, "If Hank ever had a retreat of solitude in which to concentrate and work, he never used it. With only his guitar and a new idea, he wrote and sang his songs in the back of a car on the road, backstage at the Grand Ole Opry, or in a night club dressing room. Noisy gatherings of friends didn't bother him. When he became involved with a new song Hank was almost overbearing in his drive to complete it and get approval from those around him. 'How do you like this line? Listen to this! Would you use this melody...or this one?' On...and on...perhaps all night...maybe for several days, until a single line or simple idea unfolded into a tragedy or comedy of life as ordinary people live it."

The songs of Hank Williams are simple and sparse but they have a depth that few other songwriters have been able to capture. Within that simplicity Hank captured some profound thoughts, created intense moods, and distilled complex situations. Perhaps the real key to his genius lies in making the complex simple, or at least appear so. Hank and his songs remain easy to understand but difficult to duplicate; even years later Hank's songs capture the essence of country music.

The Songs

The Alabama Waltz

I was sad and blue
I was down hearted too
It seemed like the whole world was lost
Then I took a chance
And we happened to dance
To the tune of the Alabama waltz

Waltz, waltz,
The Alabama waltz
There all my fears and cares were lost
There in your arms
With all of your charms
We danced the Alabama waltz

All The Love I Ever Had

One time you know, I loved you true
There was nothing I wouldn't do
But you have treated me so bad
You killed all the love I ever had

You leave me alone and run around
You were the talk of the town
It made you glad to see me sad
You killed all the love I ever had

No one knows the torture I went through
Loving you and knowing you were untrue
It's over now and I'm so glad
You killed all the love I ever had

All these years I've sat and cried
A thousand times my poor soul died
You have treated me so bad
You killed all the love I ever had

Alone and Forsaken

We met in the springtime when blossoms unfold
The pastures were green and the meadows were gold
Our love was in flower as summer grew on
Her love, like the leaves, now has withered and gone

The roses have faded, there's frost at my door
The birds in the morning don't sing anymore
The grass in the valley is starting to die
And out in the darkness the whippoorwills cry

Alone and forsaken
by fate and by man
Oh, Lord, if you hear me,
please hold to my hand
O, please understand

Oh where has she gone to, oh, where can she be
She may have forsaken some other like me
She promised to honor to love and obey
Each vow was a plaything that she threw away

The darkness is falling, the sky has turned gray
A hound in the distance is starting to bay
I wonder, I wonder what she's thinking of
Forsaken, forgotten, without any love

Alone and forsaken
by fate and by man
Oh, Lord, if you hear me,
please hold to my hand
Oh, please understand

Angel Mine

God must have known that I was lonely
And no contentment could I find
For one day right out of heaven
He sent me you, angel mine

Now my heart is always singing
Songs of love so divine
It will never, a-get no sorrow
Since I've found you, angel mine

I could never tell the world, dear
Of your love so true and kind
Oh, how thankful I am for you
You are my life, angel mine

I just want to live and love you
Always be your clinging vine
There could never be another
Sweet as you, angel mine

There could never be another
Sweet as you, angel mine
There could never be another
As sweet as you, angel mine

The Angel of Death

In the great Book of John, you're warned of the day
When you'll be laid beneath the cold clay
The angel of death will come from the sky
And claim your poor soul when the time comes to die

When the angel of death comes down after you
Can you smile and say that you have been true?
Can you truthfully say with your dying breath
That you're ready to meet the angel of death?

When the lights all grow dim and the dark shadows creep
And when your loved ones are gathered to weep
Can you face them and say, with your dying breath
That you're ready to meet the angel of death?

When the angel of death comes down after you
Can you smile and say that you have been true?
Can you truthfully say with your dying breath
That you're ready to meet the angel of death?

Are You Building a Temple in Heaven

Around me, many are building
Temples of beauty and wealth
But what of a temple in Heaven?
Where will you live after death?

Are you building a temple in Heaven
To live in when this life is o'er?
Will you move to that beautiful city
And live with Christ evermore?

So long is the road that leads you
To that beautiful land up there
Is work on your temple completed?
Death may be lingering near

Are you building a temple in Heaven
To live in when this life is o'er?
Will you move to that beautiful city
And live with Christ evermore?

Are You Lonely Too?

Darling I'm so lonely
    here all alone
Things are not the same, dear,
    now that you are gone
Are you lonely too, my darling,
    do mem'ries make you cry
Are you sorry now,
    that we said, "good-bye"

My days are full of sorrow,
    my nights are full of tears
And there's no hope for tomorrow,
    and the weeks have turned into years
Won't you please reconsider,
    take me back in your heart
For I don't want to live
    if we're gonna stay apart

Now when you get this letter,
    if you feel the way I do
Please, hurry on back home,
    for I'll be waiting there for you

Won't you please reconsider
Take me back in your heart
For I don't wanna live

If we're gonna stay apart
Now when you get his letter
If you feel the way, I do
Please hurry on home darling
For I'll be waiting there for you

Are You Walking and A-Talking For The Lord

On your journey to the grave
Would you stop and try to save
Are you walking and a-talking for the Lord
Would you lend a helping hand
To some poor sinner man
Are you walking and a-talking for the Lord?
Are you walking and a-talking for the Lord?

Are you walking (walking, walking)
Are you talking (talking, talking)
Are you walking and a-talking for the Lord?
Are you travelling in his land
Every day and every night
Are you walkin' and a talking for the lord?

If your heart said "testify,"
Would the world hear your reply
Are you walking and a-talking for the Lord?
Would you stand and shout His name
Or bow your head in shame
Are you walking and a-talking for the Lord?

Are you walking (are you walking)
Are you talking (are you talking)
Are you walking and a-talking for the Lord?
Are you traveling in His light

Every day and every night
Are you walking and a-talking for the Lord?

When he says come home to me
Will your soul be clean and free
Are you walking and a-talking for the Lord
When the time has come to go,
Will your road be white as snow
Are you walking and a-talking for the Lord?

Are you walking (walking, walking)
Are you talking (talking, talking)
Are you walking and a-talking for the Lord?
Are you travelling in his land?
Every day and every night
Are you walkin' and a talking for the Lord?

Baby We're Really in Love

If you're lovin' me like I'm lovin' you,
Baby we're really in love
If you're happy with me like I'm happy with you
Old Cupid just gave us a shove
If you're thinkin' of me like I'm thinkin' of you
Then I know what you're thinkin' of
If you're lovin' me like I'm lovin' you,
Baby, we're really in love

I run around in circles
And turn in fire alarms
I'm nutty as a fruitcake
When you're not in my arms

If you're meant for me like I'm meant for you
Baby we fit like a glove
If you're lovin' me like I'm lovin' you,
Baby, we're really in love

If you're lovin' me like I'm lovin' you,
Baby, we're really in love
If you're countin' on me like I'm countin' on you,
Old Cupid just gave us a shove
If you're dreamin' of me like I'm dreamin' of you,
Then I know what you're dreamin' of
If you're lovin' me like I'm lovin' you,
Baby, we're really in love

My folks think I've gone crazy
And I don't feel too sure
And yet there's nothin' wrong with me
That weddin' bells won't cure

If you go for me like I go for you,
Baby, we fit like a glove
If you're lovin' me like I'm lovin' you,
Baby, we're really in love

Bayou Pon Pon

There's a place I know you'll want to go
If you're ever feeling low
For the happiest place beneath the sun
Is Saturday night on Bayou Pon Pon

Oh the fiddles ring and the guitars sing
They have no thought of care or pain
It's time to dance, their work is done
It's Saturday night on Bayou Pon Pon

Oh sweet Marie, she'll dance with me
And such a sight you'll never see
Terese, Annette and Jole Blon will all be there
On Bayou Pon Pon

At the jamboree in Saint Landry
They have a good time, oh yes, oui oui
Point Coupe, Saint Charles, Saint James, Saint John
It's Saturday night on Bayou Pon Pon

In old Terre Bonne and bon La Fayette
Oh, the Bayou country I'll never forget
From the beautiful Teche down to Gueyden
They'll all be there on Bayou Pon Pon

Blue Is My Heart

Blue is my heart, blue as the sky
Memories of you, they're making me cry
Longing for you in days all gone by
Blue is my heart, blue as the sky

Life is so bare since you said goodbye
There's no tomorrow so why should I try
Joys of this life, they're passing me by
Blue is my heart, blue as the sky

Flower's stop bloomin', fields used to be green
Your love's just a memory, gone like the spring
Lord, come and take me away, I'm so blue everyday

Oh, my love it ain't nothing to you anymore
Sweet darling, I'm praying you'll knock at my door
Until that day comes and tears in my eyes
Blue is my heart, blue as sky
Blue is my heart, blues as the sky

The Blues Come Around

Once I was happy as I could be
But I let a gal make a fool out of me
And ever since she let me down
The blues come around when the sun goes down

Oh, the blues come around
      Yes, the blues come around
      Lawd, the blues come around
      Every evenin' when the sun goes down

Long as the sun is in the sky
These doggone blues never make me cry
But ever since she left this town,
The blues come around when the sun goes down

      [Repeat Chorus]

I built my castles very high
And then she went and said goodbye
And ever since she tore 'em down
The blues come around when the sun goes down

      [Repeat Chorus]

Once she called me all her own
But now she's gone and I'm alone
And every evenin' I'm sorrow bound
Cause the blues come around when the sun goes down

      [Repeat Chorus]

Cajun Baby

Way down yonder in the bayou country
In dear old Lousianne
There's where lives my Cajun baby
The fairest one in the land
Her teeth are white and pearly
Hair black as gold
Wouldn't trade my Cajun baby
For the world's gold
Way down yonder in the Bayou country
In dear old Lousianne

My heart's been sad and lonely
Since the day I left her side
But today I got her letter
Said she'd be my Cajun bride
Gonna go and wed my Cajun baby
And live by the old bayou
Eat a lot of shrimp and crawfish
Ride around in my old pirogue

[Repeat Chorus]

Before the sun goes down this evening
I'll be on my way
To see my Cajun baby
And there I'm gonna stay
On a Saturday night we go dancin'

And listen to the fiddle-o

Lord, I got me a Cajun baby

Just a-livin' and a-lovin' by the old bayou

[Repeat Chorus]

California Zephyr

From the great Salt Lakes of Utah
To California's golden shore
Colorado and Nevada
Through the desert's burning door
While she's circling thru the canyons,
Can't you see that mountain stream
It's the California Zephyr,
  the Union Pacific Queen

See her rocking, see her rolling
As she rambles on her way
She left L.A. this morning,
Burning up the right of way
In the distance hear her moaning,
Hear her lonesome whistle scream
It's the California Zephyr,
  the Union Pacific Queen

She leaves the City of the Angels,
Heading for ol' Santa Fe
She's making knots, she's making time,
Just watch her swing and sway
And from 'way out in the darkness,
Can't you see that headlight gleam
It's the California Zephyr,
  the Union Pacific Queen

From the great Salt Lakes of Utah
To California's golden shore
Colorado and Nevada,
Through the desert's burning door
While she's circling thru the canyons,
Can't you see that mountain stream
It's the California Zephyr,
      the Union Pacific Queen

Calling You

When you've strayed from the fold
And there's trouble in your soul
Can't you hear the blessed Savior calling you?
When your soul is lost in sin
And you're at your journey's end
Can't you hear the blessed Savior calling you?

Calling you (calling you)
Can't you hear the blessed Savior calling you?
He will take you by the hand
Lead you through that promised land
Can't you heart the blessed Savior calling you?

As you journey day by day
And temptation comes your way
Can't you hear the blessed Savior calling you?
If you follow in His light,
He will always guide you right
Can't you hear the blessed Savior calling you?

Calling you, calling you
Can't you hear the blessed Savior calling you?
If you follow Him each day
He will brighten up your way
Can't you hear the blessed Savior calling you?

When your soul is burdened down
And friends cannot be found
Can't you hear the blessed Savior calling you?
If you'll follow Him each day
He will brighten up your way
Can't you hear the blessed Savior calling you?

Calling you (calling you)
Calling you (calling you)
Can't you hear the blessed Savior calling you?
He will take you by the hand
Lead you through that promised land
Can't you heart the blessed Savior calling you?

Cold, Cold Heart

I tried so hard, my dear to show
That you're my every dream
Yet you're afraid each thing I do
Is just some evil scheme
A mem'ry from your lonesome past
Keeps us so far apart
Why can't I free your doubtful mind
and melt your cold, cold heart?

Another love before my time
Made your heart sad and blue
And so my heart is paying now
For things I didn't do
In anger, unkind words are said
That makes the teardrops start
Why can't I free your doubtful mind
And melt your cold, cold heart?

You'll never know how much it hurts
To see you sit and cry
You know you need and want my love
Yet you're afraid to try
Why do you run and hide from life
To try it just ain't smart
Why can't I free your doubtful mind
And melt your cold, cold heart?

There was a time when I believed
That you belonged to me
But now I know your heart is shackled to a memory
The more I learn to care for you
The more we drift apart
Why can't I free your doubtful mind
And melt your cold, cold heart?

Countryfied

Now most folks think I'm countryfied
And, brother, they're sure right
Cause I learned to walk behind a mule
And to read by a kerosene light
Some folks even call us fools and make fun of our ways
Cause we hang gourds on our fence posts
To keep up with the days

I'm proud to be called countrified,
Makes me happy as can be
And, friend I'm here to tell you now,
There'll be no change in me
We work our land the whole week long
But when Saturday rolls around
There ain't no keepin' us on the farm,
That's when country goes to town

Now country ham and turnip greens,
That's somethin' fit to eat
And I just don't feel comfortable
'less I'm ridin' on a wagon seat
God gave me land to make my bread
And air to breath so free
Go on and call me countryfied,
You shore ain't sland'rin me

Just one thing more I'll be forced to say
Before I head for home
I'm proud to be a country man
Cause that's where I belong
And if I treat my neighbor right
And to my God I'm true
There's one thing that I surely know
I'll get to Heaven just as quick as you

Dear Brother

Dear Brother, Mama left us this morning
Deaths angels took her away
She's gone to meet Daddy up there in Heaven
But we'll meet again some day

She left this world with a smile on her face
Whisp'ring the Savior's name
Dear brother, Mama left us this morning
For the city where there is no pain

As I stood by her bedside those last few moments
I lived my childhood again
I tho't of you, brother, and of the old homestead
And my tears they fell like rain

She left this world with a smile on her face
Whisp'ring the Savior's name
Dear brother, Mama left us this morning
For the city where there is no pain

Everything's Okay

I went to the country just the other day
To see my Uncle Bill and sorta pass the time away
I asked him how he'd been since last I'd passed his way
He rubbed his chin and here's what he had to say

My wife's been sick and the young'uns too
And I'm darn near down with the flu
The cow's gone dry and the hens won't lay
But we're still a-livin', so everything's okay

The hogs took the cholera and they've all done died
The bees got mad and they left the hive
The weevils got the corn and the rain rotted the hay
But we're still a-livin', so everything's okay

The porch rotted down, that's more expense
The durned old mule, he tore down the fence
The mortgage is due and I can't pay
But we're still a-livin', so everything's okay

The cow broke in the field and ate up the beans
The durn rabbits, they got the turnip greens
And my Maw-in-law just moved in to stay
But we're still a-livin', so everything's okay

My land's so poor, so hard and yeller,
You have to sit on a sack of fertilizer to raise an umbrella

And it rains out here nearly every day
But we're still a-livin', so everything's okay

The well's gone dry and I have to tote the water
Up from the spring about a mile and a quarter
My helper, he quit for lack of pay
But we're still a-livin', so everything's okay

The house it leaks, it needs a new top
When it rains it wets everything we got
The chimney fell down just the other day
But we're still a-livin', so everything's okay

The corn meal's gone and the meat's run out
Got nothing to kill to put in the smokehouse
The preacher's coming Sunday to spend the day
But we're still a-livin'', so everything's okay

The canned stuff's spoiled or else the jars got broke
And all we got left over is one old Billy goat
We're gonna have a new baby 'bout the first of May
But we're still a-livin', so everything's okay

My crop it rotted in the ground
I asked for another loan but the banker turned me down
But we're still a-livin', and prayin' for better days
So, after all, everything's in pretty good shape

For Me There Is No Place

You have always wanted
The finest things in life
So that all your dreams could come true
I've slaved with all my might

But the plans I made for you and me
Have all gone to waste
Cause in the world you live now
For me there is no place

Gone is the sweet and simple girl
That I have loved so long
And in her place a stranger lives
Who wants a dream world and not a home

With the sunrise I'll be gone
And then, Darling, you'll be free
Free to live the life you want
And never be bothered by me

For I am just the simple boy
Who couldn't keep up the pace
Cause in the world you live now
For me there is no place

Forever's a Long, Long Time

You swear your love will last forever
That I can always call you mine
Before we make our vows to God, dear
Forever's a long, long time

Will you always love my trusting heart, dear
Or will you some day make it pine
The years may lead you to another
Forever's a long, long time

Forever's a long, long time, my darling
Are you sure that time won't change your mind?
Are you certain your love won't grow cold, dear?
Forever's a long, long time

Unwanted hearts will fade and die, dear
For them the sun don't ever shine
So please be sure of what you're saying
Forever's a long, long time

The Funeral

I was walking in Savannah past a church, decayed and dim
When slowly through the window came a plaintive funeral hymn
And my sympathy awakened, and a wonder quickly grew
'Till I found myself enviered in a little colored pew

Out front a colored couple sat in sorrow, nearly wild
On the altar was a casket, and in the casket was a child
I could picture him while living, curly hair, protruding lips
I'd seen perhaps a thousand in my hurried southern trips

Rose a sad old colored preacher from his little wooden desk
With a manner sorta awkward, and countenance grotesque
The simplicity and shrewdness in his Ethiopian face
Showed the wisdom and ignorance of a crushed, undying race

And he said, "Now don't be weeping for this pretty bit of clay
For the little boy who lived there has done gone and run away

He was doing very finely, and he 'preciates your love
But his sho' 'nuff Father wanted him in the big house up above
The Lord didn't give you that baby, by no hundred thousand miles
He just thinks you need some sunshine, and He lent him for awhile

And He let you keep and love him 'till your hearts were bigger grown
And these silver tears you're shedding now is just interest on the loan
Just think, my poor dear mourners, creeping long on sorrow's way
What a blessed picnic this here baby got today

Your good fathers and good mothers crowd the little fellow around
In the angel's tender garden of the big plantation ground

And his eyes they brightly sparkled at the pretty things he viewed
But a tear came, and he whispered, "I want my parents, too"
But then the angel's chief musicians teached that little boy a song
Says if only they be faithful they'll soon be coming 'long

So, my poor dejected mourners, let your hearts with Jesus rest
And don't go to criticizing the One what knows the best
For He hath given many comforts, he's got the right to take away
To the Lord be praised in glory, now and ever, let us pray

Heaven Holds All My Treasures

Some people struggle for riches
And all of the things they will buy
But all of my hopes for treasures
Are away beyond the sky

Heaven holds all my treasures
More precious than diamonds or gold
Up there I'll meet my darlin'
Whom God has called back to the fold

In this world I'm just a drifter
I know nothing but sorrow and care
But to me somehow it don't matter
For I know she is waiting up there

I stand on the banks of the river
And I stare at the water so deep
And think of my darlin'
Then I bow my head and weep

Help Me Understand

A little girl prayed at the close of the day
Cause her Daddy had gone far away
On her little face was a look of despair,
I stood there and listened and I heard this prayer

My Mommy says Daddy has brought us to shame,
I'm never no more to mention his name
Lord, take me and lead me and hold to my hand--
Oh, Heavenly Father, help me understand

You know, friends, I wonder just how many homes are broken
tonight,
Just how many tears are shed by some little word of anger that
never should have been said
I'd like to tell you a story of a family I once knew
We'll name them Mary and William and their little daughter, Sue
Now Mary was just a plain Mother, and Bill and was just a usual
Dad
And they had their family quarrels, like everyone else--but neither
one got mad
Then one day something happened--it was nothing, of course
But one word led to another, and the last word led to a divorce
Now here were two grown up people who failed to see common sense
They strengthened their own selfish pride--at little Sue's expense
You know, she didn't ask to be brought into this world to drift
from pillar to post
But a divorce never stops to consider the one it hurts the most

There'd be a lot more honest lovin' in this wicked ole world today
If just a few parted parents could hear little Sue say
My Mommy says Daddy has brought us to shame,
I'm never no more to mention his name
Lord, take me and lead me and hold to may hand--
Oh, Heavenly Father, help me understand

Hey, Good Lookin'

Hey, hey good lookin', whatcha got cookin'
How's about cookin' somethin' up with me

Hey, sweet baby, don't you think maybe
We could find us a brand new recipe

I got a hot rod Ford and a two dollar bill
And I know a spot right over the hill
There's soda pop and the dancin's free
So if you wanna have fun come along with me

Hey, hey good lookin', whatcha got cookin'
How's about cookin' somethin' up with me

I'm free and ready so we can go steady
How's about savin' all your time for me

No more lookin', I know I've been tooken
How's about keepin' steady company

I'm gonna throw my date book over the fence
And find me one for five or ten cents
I'll keep it 'til it's covered with age
Cause I'm writin' your name down on every page

Hey, hey good lookin', whatcha got cookin'
How's about cookin' somethin' up with me

Home in Heaven

Around me many are building
> Homes of beauty and wealth
But what of a home in Heaven
> Where you will live after death

Are you building a home in Heaven
> To live in when this life is o'er
Will you move to that beautiful city
> And live with Christ evermore?

Long is the road that leads you
> To that beautiful home up there
Is work on your home completed?
> Death may be lingering near

Are you ready for His coming?
> Have you been true all along?
Have you finished your building in Glory?
> Will you move to your Heavenly home?

Homesick

Mean old trouble
Is all that I've known
I'm missing my honey
And boys, I'm going home
If she'll just let me tarry
When I come dragging in
You couldn't take a shotgun
And run me off again

Homesick and lonely,
I'm worried and blue
I want to see the baby
And the baby's mama, too
I'm so tired of roaming,
I'm about to lose my mind
Homesick and lonesome
For that girl of mine

This old boy's got misery
Deep down in his soul
This old world's too big,
And this old world's too cold
I'll be riding that freight train
When she comes down the track
And next time you see me leave,
I'll be flat on my back

I never knew a body
Could ever feel so low
I have often asked myself,
Why did I ever go?
I'm heading home
And there I'm gonna park
And if she wants a new dog,
Then I'm gonna learn to bark

Honey, Do You Love Me, Huh?

Honey, won't you hold me tight
Honey, won't you hold me tight
That old moon above
Was just made for love
Honey, won't you hold me tight

Start your turtle dovin',
I need a little lovin'
Honey, won't you hold me tight
Honey, do you love me, huh?
Honey, do you love me, huh?

Do you want to marry?
Got no time to tarry
Honey, do you love me, huh?
Quit your hesitating,
I'm tired of waiting
Honey, do you love me, huh?

Honky Tonk Blues

Well, I left my home down on the rural route
I told my paw I'm goin' steppin' out
And get the honky tonk blues,
Yeah, the honky tonk blues
Lord, I got 'em, I got the honky tonk blues

Well, I went to dance, wore out my shoes,
Woke up this mornin', wishin' I could lose
Them jumpin' honky tonk blues
Yeah, the honky tonk blues
Lord, I'm sufferin' with the honky tonk blues

I stopped into every place in town,
This city life has really got me down
I got the honky tonk blues,
I got the honky tonk blues
Lord, I'm sufferin' with honky tonk blues

When I get home again to Ma and Pa,
I know they're gonna lay down the law
About the honky tonk blues,
The jumpin' honky tonk blues
Lord, I'm sufferin' with the honky tonk blues

Gonna tuck my worries underneath my arm
And get right back to my Pappy's farm
And leave the honky tonk blues,
Forget the honky tonk blues
I don't want to be bothered
With the honky tonk blues

Honky Tonkin'

When you are sad and lonely
and have no place to go
Just come to see me baby
and bring along some dough
And we'll go honky tonkin'
     honky tonkin'
Honky tonkin'
     honey baby
We'll go honky tonkin' round this town

When you and your baby
have a fallin' out
Jus' call me up sweet mama
and we'll go steppin' out
And we'll go honky tonkin'
     honky tonkin'
Honky tonkin'
     honey baby
We'll go honky tonkin' round this town

We're goin' to the city,
to the city fair
If you go to the city
baby, you will find me there
And we'll go honky tonkin'
     honky tonkin'

Honky tonkin'
　　　honey baby
We'll go honky tonkin' round this town

And we'll go honky tonkin'
　　　honky tonkin'
Honky tonkin'
　　　honey baby
We'll go honky tonkin' round this town

A House of Gold

People steal, they cheat and lie
For wealth and what it will buy
But don't they know on the Judgment Day
That their gold and silver will melt away

I'd rather be in a deep, dark grave
And know that my poor soul was saved
Than to live in this world in a house of gold
And deny my God and doom my soul

Jesus said, come on to me
I'll break sin's chains and set you free
I'll carry you to a home on high
Where you'll never, never die

What good is gold and silver too
If your heart's not pure and true
Sinner, hear me when I say
Fall down on your knees and pray

Jesus died there on the cross
So this world would not be lost
Sinner hear now what I say
For someday you'll have to pay

What good is gold and silver too
If your heart's not pure and true
Sinner, hear me when I say
Fall down on your knees and pray

A House Without Love

For years we both have lived on pride, dear
And we agree that love is gone
Why, oh why do we keep trying
A house without love is not a home

The lovelight in your eyes has faded
And I'm contented just to roam
We slaved to gain a worthless treasure
A house without love is not a home

No matter where our footsteps wander
I know we'll both be all alone
With the pride that came between us
A house without love is not a home

The simple things have gone forever
We wanted wealth to call our own
And now we've reached the hour of parting
A house without love is not a home

How Can You Refuse Him Now

There's a story old
That often has been told
  of how our Savior died
As they nailed his hands
He cried "They don't understand"
  as the blood flowed down his side

As he hung there on the tree,
He prayed for you and me
  there was no one his pain to ease
Before He died,
He faintly cried
  "Father, forgive them please"

How can you refuse Him now?
How can you refuse Him now?
  How can you turn away from His side,
  With tears in His eyes
  On the Cross where He died?
How can you refuse Jesus now?

How Many Times Have You Broken My Heart?

Time after time you've proven untrue
Leavin' me home to cry over you
Each time you come back, say I'm your sweetheart
But how many times, dear, have you broken my heart?

Night after night I've cried over you
Hopin' and prayin' someday you'd be true
You took my world, tore it apart
How many times have you broken my heart?

You promised, darlin' to be just mine
But now I know that was one of your lies
You've been untrue right from the start
But how many times have you broken my heart?

Night after night I've cried over you
Hopin' and prayin' someday you'll be true
You took my world, tore it apart
How many times have you broken my heart?

Night after night I've cried over you
Hopin' and prayin' someday you'll be true
You took my world, tore it apart
Oh, how many times have you broken my heart?

You took my world, tore it apart
How many times have you broken my heart?
How many times have you broken my heart?

Howlin' At The Moon

I know there's never been a man in the awful shape I'm in
I can't even spell my name, my head's in such a spin
Today I tried to eat a steak with a big old table spoon
You got me chasin' rabbits, walkin' on my hands
and howlin' at the moon

Well, Sug, I took one look at you and it almost drove me mad
And then I even went and lost what little sense I had
Now I can't tell the day from night, I'm crazy as a loon
You got me chasin' rabbits, pullin' out my hair
and howlin' at the moon

Each time I try to dress myself my hat looks like my coat
Today I tried to tie a sock around my silly throat
A human being can't live like this, something's got to happen soon
You got me chasin' rabbits, talkin' to myself
and howlin' at the moon

Some friends of mine asked me to go out on a huntin' spree
Cause there ain't a hound dog in this state that can hold a light to me
I ate three bones for dinner today, I tried to tree a coon
You got me chasin' rabbits and I'm scratchin" fleas
and howlin' at the moon

I rode my horse to town today and a gas pump we did pass
I pulled him up and I hollered "whoa" fill him up with gas

The man picked up a monkey wrench and, wham, he changed my
tune
You got me chasin' rabbits, spittin' out teeth
and howlin' at the moon

I never thought in this old world a fool could fall so hard
But, honey baby, when I fell, the whole world must have jarred
I think I'd quit my doggish ways if you'd take me for your groom
You got me chasin' rabbits, pickin' out rings
and howlin' at the moon

I Ain't Got Nothing But Time

Little girl, if you're feeling low
And you got no place to go
      Just give me a ring,
      Some joy I will bring
'Cause I ain't' got nothing but time

Well, I ain't got nothing but time
So, baby, if you want to shine
      If you'll take time to look,
      My number's in the book
And you can call me any time

I'm footloose and I'm fancy free
So baby, just come along with me
      Grab your dancing shoes,
      We'll go and lose the blues
'Cause I ain't got nothing but time

If you say so, babe, we'll stay all night
Don't worry 'cause I ain't got no wife
      Any time you want to go,
      Good gal, just let me know
'Cause I ain't got nothing but time

No use to sit at home and pine
And let someone trouble your mind
    Just come along with me,
    There's more fish in the sea
And I ain't' got nothing but time

Now, baby, just come on and smile
You'll find that life is still worthwhile
    If you'll just look around,
    There's lots of fellows in this town
That for you, girl, ain't got nothing but time

Lord, I ain't got nothin' but time
So baby, if you want to shine
If you take time to look
My number's in the book
And you can call me anytime

I Can't Escape From You

I've tried and tried to run and hide
To find a life that's new
But where I go I always know
I can't escape from you

A jug of wine to numb my mind
But what good does it do
The jug runs dry and I still cry
I can't escape from you

These wasted tears are souvenirs
Of a love I thought was true
Your memory is chained to me
I can't escape from you

There is no end, I can't pretend
That dreams will soon come true
A slave too long to a heart of stone
I can't escape from you

I Can't Get You Off of My Mind

Oh I can't get you off of my mind
When I try I'm just wasting my time
      Lord, I've tried and I've tried
      And all night I've cried
But I can't get you off of my mind

Didn't think you would leave me behind
But I guess you're the two-timin' kind
      Do you think that's smart
      To jump from heart to heart
When I can't get you off of my mind

[Chorus]

You believe that a new love is blind
So you fool every true love you find
      You've got stars in your eyes
      But they can't hide the lies
Oh I can't get you out of my mind

[Chorus]

I Can't Help It (If I'm Still in Love With You)

Today I passed you on the street
And my heart fell at your feet
I can't help it if I'm still in love with you

Somebody else stood by your side
And he looked so satisfied
I can't help it if I'm still in love with you

A picture from the past came slowly stealing
As I brushed your arm and walked so close to you
Then suddenly I got that old time feeling
I can't help it if I'm still in love with you

It's hard to know another's lips will kiss you
And hold you just the way I used to do
Oh, heaven only knows how much I miss you
I can't help it if I'm still in love with you

I Could Never Be Ashamed of You

Everybody says you let me down
I should be ashamed to take you 'round
Makes no difference what you used to do
Darling, I could never be ashamed of you

Maybe you were reckless yesterday
But together we can find a brighter way
In my heart I know that you'll come through
Darling, I could never be ashamed of you

All the happiness I've ever known
Came the day you said you'd be my own
And it matters not what we go through
Darling, I could never be ashamed of you

Maybe you've been cheated in the past
And perhaps those memories will always last
Even though you prove to be untrue
Darling, I could never be ashamed of you

I Don't Care (If Tomorrow Never Comes)

I don't care if tomorrow never comes
This world holds nothing for me
     I've been lonely night and day
     Ever since you went away
So I don't' care if tomorrow never comes

If tomorrow never comes and the sun don't ever shine
It won't matter with me
     For when she went away
     My world ended that day
I don't' care if tomorrow never comes

My lonely mind goes back to days that used to be
My broken heart cried out for you
     Oh if I can't have you here
     I just can't go on, my dear
So I don't care if tomorrow never comes

[REPEAT CHORUS X2]

I Heard You Crying in Your Sleep

I know you tried your best to love me
You smiled when your heart told you to weep
You tried to pretend that you were happy
But last night I heard you crying in your sleep

You gave the best years of your life, dear
And each precious vow you tried to keep
I love you so much I want you happy
But last night I heard you crying in your sleep

Your heart is yearning for an old love
With new love it's useless to compete
It hurts me to know you are unhappy
But last night I heard you crying in your sleep

You know that you are free to go, dear
And don't mind if I start to weep
I know I can never make you happy
Cause last night I heard you crying in your sleep

I Hope You Shed a Million Tears

I gave my heart and soul to you
You done me wrong for years
I hope someday you suffer too
And shed a million tears

Now I can see you clear as day
There on our wedding night
The warm glow of your heart so gay
And your eyes blue shining bright

Your lips were like a rose red wine
The stars alone can yield
My one and only valentine
My lily of the field

Then there came a stranger to our town
A man of worldly charms
Who turned our whole world upside down
And stole you from my arms

Our love was like a sacred scroll
You never did learn to read
I gave to you my heart and soul
And you left it there to bleed

I made a vow to stand by you
Down through our golden years

You broke my heart and left me blue
To shed a million tears

You said goodbye so casually
Oh, I took it hard, it's true
The Bible says forgive you
But that's something I can't do

I love you like there's no tomorrow
And found out that there's not
Your Romeo came passing through
And Cupid fired a shot

When the world was ours, your heart was mine
And our dreams were one of bliss
The days were like a winding stream
And the nights were like a kiss

So we stood before out Savior
True believers in His grace
I gave my very soul to you
And you threw it in my face

I said I'd be right there with you
When we faced our final years
I hope someday you suffer too
And shed a million tears

I hope someday you suffer too
And shed a million tears

I Just Don't Like This Kind of Livin'

I just don't like this kind of livin'
I'm tired of doin' all the givin'
  I give my all and sit and yearn
  And get no lovin' in return
And I just don't like this kind of livin'

Why do we stay together,
We always fuss and fight
You ain't never known to be wrong
And I ain't never been right

Tell me where you think we're goin',
Cause I ain't got no way of knowin'
  When things go wrong you go your way,
  You leave me here to pay and pay
And I just don't like this kind of livin'

I just don't like the things you're doin'
Your evil heart will be your ruin
  When things start runnin' smooth and free,
  You haul off and pick on me
And I just don't like this kind of livin'

They say the road of love is long,
it's rocky and it's rough
But if this road don't start to get smooth
I've traveled it long enough

Why don't you act a little older
    and get that chip off your shoulder
    I told you once, now I'll tell you twice,
    you better start to treat me nice
Cause I just don't like this kind of livin'

I've Lost the Only Love I Knew

You asked me why my heart's so sad
And why the teardrops fill my eyes
A heart can't sing that's filled with pain
how can it laugh when it cries?

I saw my dreams all fade and die
Like castles in the blue
Each dawn will bring me tears and pain
I've lost the only love I knew

Oh, life for me is useless now
It seems so empty and blue
There's no more use to try again
I'll fail in everything I do

It's hard to know you'll never have
The one you love so true
While the world's asleep I'll lay and cry
I've lost the only love I knew

I Saw the Light

I wandered so aimless, life filled with sin
I wouldn't let my dear Savior in
Then Jesus came like a stranger in the night
Praise the Lord, I saw the light

I saw the light, I saw the light
No more darkness, no more night
Now I'm so happy, no sorrow in sight
Praise the Lord, I saw the light

Just like a blind man, I wandered alone
Worries and fears I claimed for my own
Then like the blind man that God gave back his sight
Praise the Lord, I saw the light

I saw the light, I saw the light
No more darkness, no more night
Now I'm so happy, no sorrow in sight
Praise the Lord, I saw the light

I was a fool to wander a-stray
Straight is the gate and narrow the way
Now I have traded the wrong for the right
Praise the Lord, I saw the light

I saw the light, I saw the light
No more darkness, no more night
Now I'm so happy, no sorrow in sight
Praise the Lord, I saw the light

I Told a Lie to My Heart

I told my heart I didn't love you
That I'd be happy if we'd part
But now I know I was mistaken
I told a lie to my heart

I told my heart I didn't love you
Now we'll forever be apart
Lonely years of tears and sorrow
I told a lie to my heart

If we sin somehow we pay
And now the bitter teardrops start
I must learn to live without you
I told a lie to my heart

I told my heart I didn't love you
That I'd be happy if we'd part
Lonely years of tears and sorrow
I told a lie to my heart

I Watched My Dream World Crumble Like Clay

I built a dream world
Darling, for two
Built it on hope
And a love I thought was true
But I've seen my blue skies
All turn to gray
I watched my dream world
Crumble like clay

We were so happy
Darling, we two
But then you changed dear
You found someone new
I saw all the joys of life
Fade far away
I watched my dream world
Crumble like clay

You promised darling
That we'd never part
But now you've gone, dear
Breaking my heart
I saw your love dear
Fade and die away
I watched my dream world
Crumble like clay

I Wish You Didn't Love Me So Much

Well, you say "Get out and you better stay gone"
Then you have a big policeman drag me back home
You tell him good and loud "Put him in the calaboose"
Then you cry and ask the judge to turn me loose
You say, "It's cause I love you" you little such and such
I'm beginning to wish you didn't love me so much

Now my life with you has been one hard knock
My head looks like an old chopped block
I tell you right now, babe, that ain't all
You've kicked me til I feel like a used football
You say "It's cause I love you," you little such and such
I'm beginning to wish you didn't love me so much

Now the preacher man said, "For better or worse"
Lately I've been lookin' for that big black hearse
I wish to my soul you'd slow down the pace
Cause I tell you right now the hides gettin' sca'ce
You say "It's cause I love you," you little such and such
I'm beginning to wish you didn't love me so much

I used to think you were a meek little thing
But, babe, among tigers, you'd be queen
If a poor little rabbit had you on his side
Every hound in the county would crawl off and hide
You say "It's cause I love you" you little such and such
I'm beginning to wish you didn't love me so much

I Won't Be Home No More

You're just in time to be too late
I tried to, but I couldn't wait
And now I've got another date
So I won't be home no more

You're just in time to miss the boat
So don't take off your hat and coat
Be on your way, that's all she wrote
Cause I won't be home no more

I stood around a month or two
And waited for your call
Now I'm too busy pitchin' woo,
So come around next fall

I scratched your name right off my slate
And hung a sign on my front gate
"You're just in time to be too late"
And I won't be home no more

Well, you're just in time to turn around
And drive your buggy back to town
You looked me up, I turned you down
And I won't be home no more

You're just in time to change your tune
Go tell your troubles to the moon
And call around next May or June
Cause I won't be home no more

I used to be the patient kind,
Believed each alibi
But that's all done, I've changed my mind
I've got new fish to fry

You're just in time to celebrate
The thing you didn't calculate
You're just in time to be too late
And I won't be home no more

I'm Going Home

When my work here is o'er
And trials come no more
On that great day, I'm going home
To live for evermore
Just over on Heaven's shore
When my life here is 'o er I'm going home

I'm going home, I'm going home,
When my life here is o'er I'm going home
Won't it be so sweet, to rest at Jesus' feet
When my life here is o'er I'm going home

I am traveling in the light
And my way is clear and bright
Some glad day I'm going home
Heading for the pearly gates
For there my Savior waits
When my life here is o'er I'm going home

As I travel down life's road
So heavy is my load
But some glad day I'm going home
I'll meet my loved ones there
In that land so bright and fair
When my life here is o'er I'm going home

I'm going home, I'm going home,
When my life here is o'er I'm going home
Won't it be so sweet, to rest at Jesus' feet
When my life here is o'er I'm going home

I'm Not Coming Home Anymore

When you get home, there you will find
This letter dear that I have wrote to you
And when you read it oe'r
Till then you'll understand
Why I'm not coming home anymore

Oh there ain't no use to cry
Because we're saying goodbye
We have discussed that oe'r and oe'r
So you go your way to you may life be kind
For I'm not coming home anymore

Darling we were so happy and had a happy home
The baby we were so proud of you
But then you went astray
I'll never forget that day
For him to know I'd much rather be dead

When from you I'm far away I'll long for you each day
The baby I will miss him so
But from you I will go
For it's all over so
I'm not coming home anymore

I'm So Happy I Found You

The tears you see within my eyes
Don't' mean that I'm sad and blue
No one has told me of your lies
I'm cryin' 'cause I'm so happy I found you

It was sad, this heart of mine
I fail in everything I do
You love me, sunshine, I'm cryin'
'Cause I'm so happy I found you

I'll never know real happiness
The thrill of love I never knew
And since I've known your sweet caress
I'm cryin"'cause I'm so happy I found you

Each night I kneel down dear and pray
And thank God for your love so true
I'm thankful that you came my way
I'm cryin' 'Cause I'm so happy I found you
I'm cryin' 'cause I'm so happy I found you

I'd Still Want You

I could shame you 'til you hide your face
And drag you right down in disgrace
But what good would it do,
     I know I'd still want you

I could tell the world you're doin' wrong
That I was stringin' you along
And if it all were true,
     I know I'd still want you

The world with me might sympathize
When I got thru with all my lies
But I'd be just as blue,
     My heart would still want you

I could tell my friends I threw you down
And slander you all over town
But what good would it do,
     I know I'd still want you

If I said I'm happy to be free
The only one I'd fool is me
Because it isn't true,
     I know I'd still want you

What's the use to say that you're no good
When I'd crawl back if I could
No matter what you do,
      I know I'd still want you

If the things I said should break your heart
And folks looked down on you
I'd be the first to take your part
      And say it wasn't true

I could smile and say I don't care
And then go home and pull my hair
But what good would it do?
      I know I'd still want you

I could say that someone put me wise
And get revenge by telling lies
But when I got all thru
      I know I'd still want you
If the things, I said was to break your heart
I'd be the first to take your part
'Cause if all these lies were true
I know I'd still want you

I'll Be a Bachelor 'Til I Die

I'll take you to the picture show
And baby I'll hold your hand
I'll sit up in your parlor,
Let you cool me with your fan
I'll listen to your troubles
And pet you when you cry
But get that marryin' out of your head,
      I'll be a bachelor 'til I die

I don't mind honky tonkin' 'round
If that will bring you fun
But somehow I can't understand
How one and one make one
I like to cuddle near you
And listen to you lie
But get that marryin' out of your head,
      I'll be a bachelor 'til I die

Now if you want a help-mate,
You're wasting lots of time
Cause I'm afraid of church bells,
How they scare me when they chime
I've seen those married people
Just up and say good-bye
So get that marryin' out of your head,
      I'll be a bachelor 'til I die

This freedom's mighty precious
In this land of liberty
I've seen what matrimony
Done to better men than me
I don't mind keepin' company
With the apple of my eye
But keep that marryin' out of your head,
  I'll be a bachelor 'til I die

I'll Never Get Out of This World Alive

Now you're lookin' at a man that's gettin' kind of mad
I've had a lot of luck but it's all been bad
No matter how I struggle and strive
I'll never get out of this world alive

My fishin' pole is broke, the creek is full of sand
My woman ran away with another man
No matter how I struggle and strive
I'll never get out of this world alive

A distant uncle passed away and left me quite a batch
And I was livin' high until that fatal day
A lawyer proved I wasn't born, I was only hatched

Everything's again' me and it's got me down
If I jumped in the river I would probably drown
No matter how I struggle and strive
I'll never get out of this world alive

These shabby shoes I'm wearin' all the time
Are full of holes and nails
And brother, if I stepped on a worn out dime,
I bet a nickel I could tell if it was heads or tails

I'm not gonna worry wrinkles in my brow
Cause nothin's ever gonna be alright no how
No matter how I struggle and strive
I'll never get out of this world alive

I could buy a Sunday suit and it would leave me broke
If it had two pair of pants I would burn the coat
No matter how I struggle and strive
I'll never get out of this world alive

If it was rainin' gold I wouldn't stand a chance
I wouldn't have a pocket in my patched up pants
No matter how I struggle and strive
I'll never get out of this world alive

I'm a Long Gone Daddy

All you want to do is sit around and pout
And now I got enough and so I'm gettin' out
I'm leavin' now, I'm leavin' now
I'm a long gone daddy, I don't need you anyhow

I've been in the doghouse for so doggone long
That when I get a kiss I think that something's wrong
I'm leavin' now, I'm leavin' now
I'm a long gone daddy, I don't need you anyhow

I'll go find a gal that wants to treat me right
You go and get yourself a man that wants to fight
I'm leavin' now, I'm leavin' now
I'm a long gone daddy, I don't need you anyhow

You start your jaws a-waggin' and they never stop
You never shut your mouth until I blow my top
I'm leavin' now, I'm leavin' now
I'm a long gone daddy, I don't need you anyhow

I remember back when you were nice and sweet
Now things have changed, you'd rather fight than eat
I'm leavin' now, I'm leavin' now
I'm a long gone daddy, I don't need you anyhow

I'm gonna do some ridin' on the midnight train
I'm taking everything except my ball and chain
I'm leavin' now, I'm leavin' now
I'm a long gone daddy, I don't need you anyhow

I'm Gonna Sing

When I get to glory
I'm gonna sing, sing, sing
I'm gonna let the hallelujahs ring
I'm gonna praise my blessed Savior's name
When I get to glory
I'm gonna sing, sing, sing

In this world of sorrow,
I've seen trouble and woe
When I get to glory,
I'll see no more
For I know my prayers
Have not been in vain
When I get to glory,
I'm gonna sing, sing sing

Sometimes I get so weary inside
Then I recall how my Jesus died
Up there I know there'll be no pain
When I get to glory,
I'm gonna sing, sing, sing

When I get to glory
I'm gonna sing, sing, sing
I'm gonna let the hallelujahs ring
I'm gonna praise my blessed Savior's name
When I get to glory
I'm gonna sing, sing, sing

Up there no tears will blind my eyes
And I'll walk along by my Jesus' side
I'll meet my loved ones all once again
When I get to glory,
I'm gonna sing, sing, sing

When I get to glory
I'm gonna sing, sing, sing
I'm gonna let the hallelujahs ring
I'm gonna praise my blessed Savior's name
When I get to glory
I'm gonna sing, sing, sing

I'm Just Crying Cause I Care

You were my every dream come true
But your love I can never share
A heart can't smile if it's filled with tears
Now, I'm just crying 'cause I care

I'm crying cause your love is gone
My burden seems more than I can bear
I saw my angel pass me by
Now, I'm just crying 'cause I care

Your eyes were like the heavens blue
Your heart I thought so true and fair
Still you'll always be mine in dreams
Now, I'm just crying 'cause I care

May all the dreams you dream come true
This will be my daily prayer
May life reserve for you the best
I'm just crying 'cause I care
Now, I'm just crying 'cause I care

I'm So Lonesome I Could Cry

Hear that lonesome whippoorwill
He sounds too blue to fly
The midnight train is whining low
I'm so lonesome I could cry

I've never seen a night so long
When time goes crawling by
The moon just went behind the clouds
To hide its face and cry

Did you ever see a robin weep
When leaves begin to die
That means he's lost the will to live
I'm so lonesome I could cry

The silence of a falling star
Lights up a purple sky
And as I wonder where you are
I'm so lonesome I could cry

I'm So Tired of It All

All my life I've been so lonesome
     If happiness came, I missed the call
All my dreams have died and vanished
     And now, I'm so tired of it all

In life and love I've been a failure
     Too many tears thru it all
Too many broken vows and promises
     And now, I'm so tired of it all

Everything I've loved, I've lost it
     Too many times I've watched my castles fall
My life is full of regretting
     And now, I'm so tired of it all

From this world I'll soon be going
     No one will miss me after all
Up there, I know I'll find contentment
     For here, I'm so tired of it all

I'm Sorry For You My Friend

You've known so long that you were wrong
But still you had your way
You told her lies and alibis
And hurt her more each day
But now your conscience bothers you,
You've reached your journey's end
You're asking me for sympathy,
I'm sorry for you, my friend

You laughed inside each time she cried,
You tried to make her blue
She tagged along thru right and wrong
Because she worshipped you
You know that you're the one to blame,
There's no use to pretend
Today's the day, you start to pay,
I'm sorry for you my friend

Today as she walked arm in arm
At someone else's side
It made you stop and realize
That time has turned the tide
You should have known you'd be alone
Cause cheaters never win
You tried and lost, now pay the cost,
I'm sorry for you, my friend

I've Been Down That Road Before

Now friend, if you'll just listen to me you'll get some good, hard earned advice
I don't aim to meddle in your business, just tryin' to save you an awful price

You see these teeth, I ain't got and these knots on my bald head?
I'll guarantee you boys, I didn't get them a-lyin' home in bed

Now, take the smart aleck in any town, of him folks want no part
He acts like his head was only made to hold his ears apart

Now, he might not like what I'm 'bout to say and my words may make him sore
But I'm just tryin' to be helpful, cause I've been down that road before

To bully folks and play mean tricks was once my pride and joy
'Till one day I was toted home and Mama didn't know her little boy

My head was swelled up so doggone big I couldn't get it through my front door
Now, I ain't just talkin' to hear myself, I've been down that road before

A little fellow about my size got tired of being pushed about
So he went to work and when he got through, he'd knocked every

one of my teeth out
One time too many I'd rubbed him wrong and he evened up the
score
Now that's what happens when you get too big for your britches,
I've been down that road before

Now when you get to thinkin' you're really smart, there's somebody
smarter than you
And no matter how much you boast and brag, you can still learn
a thing or two
Go get you some treatments just like I've had and you won't hanker
for more
I really learned the meaning of living and loving, I been down that
road before

Now the man that walks this rocky road usually gets just what he
deserves
Cause he's just a helpless servant to a master that he serves
Now I've learned to slow my temper down and not to pick no
scraps no more
Boys, it's a lot easier on the heads and eyes, I've been down that
road before

If I Didn't Love You

If I didn't love you
I wouldn't be so lonesome
And I'd never cry over you
If I didn't love you
I wouldn't be jealous
Cause I wouldn't care what you do

People are saying
That you'll let me down
But I know someday you'll come through
If I didn't love you
I wouldn't be so lonesome
Waiting and longing for you

If I didn't love you
I wouldn't be pining
My heart out the way that I do
If I didn't love you
I wouldn't be wond'ring
Who's sharing this moment with you

Time after time
I have proved that I care
I've tried to be faithful and true
If I didn't love you
I wouldn't be lonesome
Waiting and longing for you

If You'll Be a Baby (To Me)

I'll be your baby
And I don't mean maybe
If you'll be a baby to me
I'll be your darlin'
And there'll be no quarrelin'
If you'll be a baby to me
'Cause I can plow and milk the cow
Even do the churnin'
You just look through your cook book
And keep the home fires burning
'Cause baby, I'll be your baby
If you'll be a baby to me

I'll be your honey,
Let you spend my money
If you'll be a baby to me
I'll be our dandy
And I'll bring you candy
If you'll be a baby to me
'Cause I can work and pay the bills
And make believe it thrills me
You can bake a choc'late cake
And I'll eat it if it kills me
Baby, I'll be your baby
If you'll be a baby to me

In My Dreams You Still Belong To Me

Now at last you've gone and left me
Like a piece of driftwood on the sea
You said that you no longer loved me
But in my dreams you still belong to me

In my dreams you're still my only darlin'
Just like you used to be
And though I've lost you to another
In my dreams you still belong to me

At night when I am sad and lonely
It's then I really know you're gone
But I just go to sleep praying
That you'll be back before so long

No matter where you wander, darlin'
If it be across the deep blue sea
Everyday you'll know I'll miss you
And in my dreams you'll still belong to me

In my dreams you're still my only darlin'
Just like you used to be
And though I lost you to another
In my dreams you still belong to me

Is This Goodbye?

Well you say we are through and for me to move on
But tell me, sweet mama, will you cry when I'm gone
Are you sure you mean it when you tell me to fly?
What I want to know, is this goodbye?

Oh, after I leave you will you follow me around
Fightin' and fussin' all over this town
Are you gonna be happy or will you cry?
What I want to know, is this goodbye?

Now, you know you've said this many times before
When your money runs out, you're bangin' on my door
Are you gonna be good or try to black my eye?
What I want to know, is this goodbye?

Like a stubborn mule always changin' your mind
Will the weather be fair or will it rain all the time?
Will the lightning strike when me'n my blonde walk by?
What I want to know, is this goodbye?

Now baby you know I always aim to please
For I want your little heart to be at ease
I don't want no dynamite fallin' from the sky
What I want to know, is this goodbye?

Jambalaya (On The Bayou)

Goodbye Joe, me gotta go, me oh my oh
Me gotta go pole the pirogue down the bayou
My Yvonne, the sweetest one, me oh my oh
Son of a gun, we'll have big fun on the bayou

Thibodaux, Fontaineaux, the place is buzzin'
Kinfolk come to see Yvonne by the dozen
Dress in style, go hog wild, me oh my oh
Son of a gun, we'll have big fun on the bayou

Jambalaya and a crawfish pie and fillet gumbo
'Cause tonight I'm gonna see ma cher amio
Pick guitar, fill fruit jar and be gay-o
Son of a gun, we'll have big fun on the bayou

Settle down far from town, get me a pirogue
And I'll catch all the fish in the bayou
Swap my mon to buy Yvonne what she need-o
Son of a gun, we'll have big fun on the bayou

Jambalaya and a crawfish pie and fillet gumbo
'Cause tonight I'm gonna see ma cher amio
Pick guitar, fill fruit jar and be gay-o
Son of a gun, we'll have big fun on the bayou

Jesus Died For Me

When everything goes wrong
And it seems all hope is gone
I remember how my Savior died
He died there on the cross
So this world would not be lost
Jesus died for me long ago

Jesus died for me long ago
On a hillside far away
He was tortured and slain
God bless His holy name

Jesus died for me long ago
What pain He suffered there,
The Holy One so dear
So that you and I could live
I'll try to repay
For His suffering on that day
Jesus died for me long ago

Jesus died for me long ago
On a hillside far away
He was tortured and slain
God bless His holy name

Jesus died for me long ago
As he hung there all alone
His life's blood almost gone
He never stopped praying for me
So I'll follow all the way
And live with Him someday
Jesus died for me long ago

Jesus died for me long ago
On a hillside far away
He was tortured and slain
God bless His holy name

Jesus Is Calling

When your soul is weary
And it seems you've lost your way
Jesus is calling,
        calling night and day
When you need a friend
To go with you all the way
Jesus is calling,
        calling night and day

Jesus is calling,
        calling night and day
And you will hear Him
if you'll just pray
Calling for you (my brother)
Don't turn away (from Jesus)
Jesus is calling
        calling night and day

If you're lost in sin,
There's no need for you to stay
Jesus is calling,
        calling night and day
If the night is dark,
You will soon see the day
Jesus is calling,
calling night and day

Jesus Remembered Me

I was all alone and drifting
On a lonely sea of sin
Nothing but darkness,
No sunshine within
I lifted my eyes
To the Lord in the skies
And Jesus remembered me

Jesus remembered me
And so He set me free
Once I was blinded but now I can see
Glory to God,
      He remembered me

Now the sun is shining,
I'm happy and free
No more sorrows,
No troubles to see
I'm going home to glory,
My Savior to see
Glory to God,
      He remembered me

Jesus remembered me
And so He set me free
Once I was blinded but now I can see
Glory to God,
      He remembered me

When He talked to His disciples
At the Sea of Galilee
He said He'd remember
A mortal like me
I asked for His blessing
Down on my knee
And Glory to God,
            He remembered me

Just Me and My Broken Heart

A careless word, a foolish quarrel
And now we are far apart
All I have left of the love we knew
Is just me and my broken heart

Joy has turned to sorrow
Smiles have turned to tears
Foolish pride has left me
With nothing but lonely years

Me and my broken heart
The time will never mend
Now we'll just live with memories
Of the one that was our only friend

Too late to say I'm sorry
To change those words I said
Too late to ask forgiveness
For another you have wed

Just Waitin'

The old maid's a-waitin' for leap year to come
The crooner's just waitin' to sing
The old cow's standin' by the Bull Durham sign
Just waitin' for the grass to turn green

The bar fly's waitin' for an easy mark
The hitchhiker's waitin" for a ride
The life termer's waitin' for a prison break
The beachcomber's waitin' for the tide

The farmer's daughter's waitin' for the salesman
To take her into town
The city slicker's waitin' for the country boy
To lay all his money down

You know, everything comes to a standstill
Nothing seems to make a turn
Worm must be waitin' for the early bird
And I guess the early bird's waitin' for the worm

Nobody wants to do nothin'
Just waitin' to get a finger in the pie
Waitin' for a call from a big quiz show
Or hopin' a-waitin' for some rich uncle to die

Katy, she's waitin' at the garden gate
The moonshiner's waitin' at the still
The gambler's waitin' for that ace in the hole
And I guess Jack's still waitin' for Jill

Everybody's waitin' for something
Nothin' seems to turn out right
'Cause the night shift's waitin' for morning
And the burglar's just waitin' for night

The congregation's waitin' for the preacher
The preacher's just waitin' for the groom
The groom's just waitin' for the June bride
And the bride's just waitin' for June

Sunflower's waitin' for the sunshine
Violets just waitin' for the dew
Bees just waitin' for the honey
And honey, I'm just waitin' for you

Kaw-Liga

Kaw-Liga was a wooden Indian
      standing by the door
He fell in love with an Indian maid
      over in the antique store
Kaw-Liga, just stood there and never let it show
So she could never answer "yes" or "no"

He always wore his Sunday feathers
      and held a tomahawk
The maiden wore her beads and braids
      and hoped some day he'd talk
Kaw-Liga, too stubborn to ever show a sign
Because his heart was made of knotty pine

Poor ol' Kaw-Liga, he never got a kiss
Poor ol' Kaw-Liga, he don't know what he missed
Is it any wonder that his face is red?
Kaw-Liga, that poor ol' wooden head

Kaw-Liga was a lonely Indian,
      never went nowhere
His heart was set on the Indian maiden
      with the coal black hair
Kaw-Liga, just stood there and never let it show
So she could never answer "yes" or "no"

Then one day a wealthy customer
        bought the Indian maid
And took her, oh, so far away
        but ol' Kaw-Liga stayed
Kaw-Liga, just stands there as lonely as can be
And wishes he were still an old pine tree

Poor ol' Kaw-Liga, he never got a kiss
Poor ol' Kaw-Liga, he don't know what he missed
Is it any wonder that his face is red?
Kaw-Liga, that poor ol' wooden head

Last Night I Dreamed of Heaven

Last night I dreamed of Heaven
And I saw my mother there
Standing with all the angels
On a golden stair
I thought I heard her whisper
"Welcome, home, my boy"
Last night I dreamed of Heaven
And it filled my heart with joy

I heard the angels singing
Songs of peace and rest
And then there was a silence
Each eye looked toward the West
There sat my Savior
On His golden throne
Last night I dreamed of Heaven
My eternal home sweet home

Last night I dreamed of Heaven
That land so pure and sweet
And the joy within me
Made my glad heart weep
I was there with my Savior
Free from grief and strife
Last night I dreamed of Heaven
The land of eternal life

Let's Turn Back the Years

Darling, let's turn back the years
And go back to yesterday
Let's pretend that time has stopped
And I didn't go away

We had our love to make us happy
It wasn't meant to bring us tears
Love like ours should never die
So, darling, let's turn back the years

Little Bocephus

Little Bocephus, you're the one, makes me feel good inside
Just to know that you're my son makes my heart swell with pride

I've always needed one like you to love and understand
Now that you've come to fill that place, you're my buddy, man
to man

There comes a time when every boy grows so cocksure with life
So that he feels he knows it all and no longer needs advice
This complicated phase of life is called "adolescent age"
And sometimes breaks a father's heart--wish you could skip
that stage

I'd like to help you fill your heart with kindness, faith and truth
Protect you from the hands that reach out to destroy manhood
and you
There is so much sorrow and despair to blight the hearts of men
And the more we learn of love and life, the more they come
crowding in

It's just little things at first, my son, then, as we older grow
Our troubles grow much bigger too and, sometimes, they overflow
Then poisoned minds and broken hearts will cause strongest
men to weep
Overwhelm souls with bitterness and death would be so sweet

So we must build a strong defense of love and fortitude
On character and knowledge, son, so these ills cannot intrude
Ah, sonny boy, so many things a youngster needs to know
If he is to find true happiness as down through this life he goes

It's just a father's love, I guess, that comes to every dad
That makes me want to shelter you from things that make you sad
Bocephus, boy, I'm standing by to help you when you call
For, son, you are my flesh and blood and the grandest pal of all

The Little House We Built (Just O'er The Hill)

It seems like only yesterday
We planned our wedding day
I loved you then and I always will
But my jealous, foolish pride
Drove me from your side
And the little house we built
  just o'er the hill

Each night I lay awake
And watch my poor heart break
For darling, your memory lingers still
And though I pray and yearn,
I know I can't return
To the little house we built
  just o'er the hill

If I should pass you on the street,
I know I couldn't speak
To see you would make my poor heart chill
For you'll welcome me no more
'Cause I have locked the door
To the little house we built
  just o'er the hill

So cry, oh lying heart,
You know you made us part
You cheated and now you'll pay the bill
She won't meet you at the gate,
For you there's only hate
In the little house we built
      just o'er the hill

I would give my life tonight
Again to hold you tight
I'm lonely as a whippoorwill
Though her love for me has gone,
She won't ever be alone
In the little house we built
      just o'er the hill

Each time I hear her name,
I bow my head in shame
For God only knows how I feel
And until He calls to me,
I'll live in memory
In the little house we built
      just o'er the hill

The Log Train

If you will listen, a song I will sing
About my Daddy who ran a log train
Way down in the southland, in ole Alabam
We lived in a place that they called Chapman Town

And late in the evening, when the sun was low
Way off in the distance you could hear the train blow
The folks would come runnin', and Mama would sing
Get the supper on the table, here comes the log train

Every mornin' at the break of day
He'd grab his lunch bucket and be on his way
Winter or summer, sunshine or rain
Every mornin' he'd run that ole log train

A-sweatin' and swearin' all day long
Shoutin,' 'Get up the oxens, keep movin' along,"
Load her up boys, cause it looks like rain
I've got to get rollin' this ole log train

This story happened a long time ago
The log train is silent, God called Dad to go
But when I get to Heaven to always remain
I'll listen for the whistle on that old log train

Long Gone Lonesome Blues

I went down to the river to watch the fish swim by
But I got to the river so lonesome I wanted to die
Oh, Lawd, and then I jumped in the river
But the doggone river was dry
She's long gone, and now I'm lonesome blue

I had me a woman, she couldn't be true
She made for my money and she made me blue
A man needs a woman that he can lean on
But my leanin' post is done left and gone
She's long gone, and now I'm lonesome blue

Gonna find me a river, one that's cold as ice
When I find me that river, Lawd, I'm gonna pay the price
Oh, Lawd I'm goin' down three times,
But I'm only coming up twice
She's long gone, and now I'm lonesome blue

She told me on Sunday she was checkin' me out
Long about Monday she was nowhere about
And here it is Tuesday, ain't had no news
I got them "gone but not forgotten" blues
She's long gone, and now I'm lonesome blue

(I Heard That) Lonesome Whistle

I was riding Number Nine
Heading south from Caroline
I heard that lonesome whistle blow

Got in trouble, had to roam
Left my gal an' left my home
I heard that lonesome whistle blow

Just a kid, acting smart
I went and broke my darling's heart
I guess I was too young to know
They took me off the Georgia Main
Locked me to a ball and chain
I heard that lonesome whistle blow

All alone, I bear the shame
I'm a number, not a name
I heard that lonesome whistle blow

All I do is sit an' cry
When the evening train goes by
I heard that lonesome whistle blow

I'll be locked here in this cell
'Till my body's just a shell
And my hair turns whiter than snow
I'll never see that gal of mine Lord,
I'm in Georgia doing time
I heard that lonesome whistle blow

Lost On the River

Lost on the river, dark is the night
Just like the blind, praying for sight
Drifting alone, heart filled with strife
I'm lost on the river,
      The river of life

Once, dear, I thought I knew the way
That was before old sad yesterday
Words that you said cut like a knife
I'm lost on the river,
      The river of life

Out on this river where sorrow creeps
Thinking of you, how my heart weeps
Tomorrow you'll be another man's wife
I'm lost on the river,
      The river of life

The Love That Faded

The love that faded left me only tears
Days that were happy turned into lonely years
Vows that we made turned into lies
My life is empty, my lonely heart cries

I tried to forget that we'll never be
Nothing left for me but dust in the breeze
My way is lonely but I think I'm lost
My love was wasted, I'm paying the cost

Brown eyes, blue eyes they're all the same
None are for me, I've lost their game
Tomorrow has nothing but worries and cares
The love that faded left me only tears

Just like the rose your love faded away
Now my lonely heart must break and pay
Nothing now but heartaches through years
The love that faded left me only tears

Low Down Blues

Lord, I went to the doctor, he took one look
He said, "The trouble with you ain't in my book"
I'll tell you what it is, but it ain't good news
You got an awful bad case of them low down blues

I got the mean old miseries in my soul
I went to the river but the water's too cold
I walked the floor till I wore out my shoes
Lord, they're killing me, I mean them low down blues

Lord, I never knew man could feel so bad
I never knew livin' could be so sad
All I do is sit and cry
Lord, I'd have to get better before I could die

I got the mean old miseries in my soul
I went to the river but the water's too cold
I walked the floor till I wore out my shoes
Lord, they're killing me, I mean them low down blues

A Mansion on the Hill

Tonight down here in the valley
I'm lonesome and oh how I feel
As I sit here alone in my cabin
I can see your mansion on the hill

Do you recall when we parted
The story to me you revealed
You said you could live without loving
In your loveless mansion on the hill

I've waited all through the years, love
To give you a heart true and real
Cause I know you're living in sorrow
In your loveless mansion on the hill

The light shines bright from your window
The trees stand so silent and still
I know you're alone with your pride, dear
In your loveless mansion on the hill

May You Never Be Alone

Like a bird that's lost its mate in flight
I'm alone and, oh so blue tonight
Like a little piece of driftwood on the sea
May you never be alone like me

I believed the lies you told to me
When you whispered, "Dear, I worship thee"
Now here am I alone and blue
All because I loved no one but you

I gave up my friends, I left my home
When you promised to be mine alone
Now you're gone, our love could never be
May you never be alone like me

In the Bible, God's own words do say
For every wrong, someday you'll pay
I pray the Lord to set me free
May you never be alone like me

Me and My Broken Heart

Oh can't you see what you have done to me
Oh, foolish, foolish pride
You brought tears and sorrow
To an untrue heart that never cried
We were waiting at the church
We stood and saw the wedding start
As the organ played, we stood there and prayed
  Just me and my broken heart

I saw the sunshine of my life
Who once, I know, just worshipped me
Standing by another's side
And soon his bride she will be
I bowed my head in grief and shame
As I felt the teardrops start
As the organ played, we stood there and prayed
  Just me and my broken heart

Men With Broken Hearts

You'll meet many just like me upon life's busy street
With shoulders stooped and heads bowed low and eyes that stare in defeat
For souls that live within the past where sorrow plays all parts
For a living death is all that's left for men with broken hearts

You have no right to be the judge, to criticize and condemn
Just think, but for the grace of God it would be you instead of him
One careless step, a thoughtless deed, and then the misery starts
And to those who weep, death comes cheap, these men with broken hearts

Humble you should be when they come passing by
For it's written that the greatest of men never get too big to cry
Some lose faith in love and life when sorrow shoots her darts
With hope all gone they walk alone, these men with broken hearts

You've never walked in that man's shoes, or saw things through his eyes
Or stood and watched with helpless hands while the heart inside you dies
Some were paupers, some were kings, and some were masters of the arts
But in their shame they're all the same, these men with broken hearts

Life sometimes can be so cruel that a heart will pray for death
God, why must these living dead know pain with every breath
So help your brother along the road, no matter where you start
For the God that made you, made them too, these men with broken hearts

Message to My Mother

Take this message to my mother
It will fill her heart with joy
Tell her that I've met my Savior
God has saved her wandering boy

The tears and sorrow I have caused her
How I wish I could repay
But tell her I'll be waiting for her
We'll meet in Heaven some glad day

How she cried when I left her
I know it filled her heart with pain
She said, "Son, please don't leave me
For we may never meet again"

Take this message to my mother
It will fill her heart with joy
Tell her that I've met my Savior
God has saved her wandering boy

Years have passed since that parting
But I know she waits and prays
Soon I'll cross that dark river
Please let her know that I was saved

Take this message to my mother
It will fill her heart with joy
Tell her that I've met my Savior
God has saved her wandering boy

Mind Your Own Business

If the wife and I are fussin', brother, that's our right
Cause me and that sweet woman's got a license to fight
Why don't you mind your own business
    Mind your own business
Cause if you mind your own business,
    you won't be mindin' mine

Oh, the woman on our party line's the nosiest thing
She picks up her receiver when she knows it's my ring
Why don't you mind your own business,
    Mind your own business
Well, if you mind your business,
    then you won't be mindin' mine

I got a little gal that wears her hair up high
The boys all whistle at her every time she walks by
Why don't you mind your own business,
    Mind your own business
Well, if you mind your business,
    Then you won't be mindin' mine

If I want to honky tonk around 'til two or three
Now brother, that's my headache, don't you worry 'bout me
Why don't you mind your own business,
    Mind your own business
Cause if you mind your business,
    You won't be mindin' mine

Mindin' other peoples' business seems to be high tone

But I got all that I can do just mindin' my own

Why don't you mind your own business,

      Mind your own business

Well if you mind your business,

      You won't be mindin' mine

Moanin' the Blues

When my baby moved out and the blues moved in,
There wasn't nothin' I could do
But mosey around with my head in my hands,
Oh, what am I comin' to
I just keep moanin'
      Moanin' the blues

I wrote a nice long letter
Sayin' Mama, please come home
Your Daddy is lonesome
      And all I do is moan

I've been lovin' that gal for so doggone long,
I can't afford to lose her now
I thoought I was right but I must have been wrong
Cause my head is startin' to bow
And now I'm moanin'
      Moanin' the blues

If you want a good gal to stay around,
You got to treat her nice and kind
If you do her wrong she'll leave this town
And you'll almost lose your mind
Then you'll be moanin'
      Moanin' the blues

Aw baby, baby, baby,
Honey baby please come home
Your Daddy is lonesome
  And all I do is moan

I promise you, baby, that I'll be good
And I'll never be bad no more
I'm sittin' here waitin' for you right now
To walk through that front door
Then I'll stop moanin'
  Moanin' the blues

Mother is Gone

In a little pine grove by the old home
There's someone who's restin' alone
And there on the tomb, these words I read
The words were, "Mother is gone"

Mother is gone to her home
Way up in Heaven above
And my heart's so sad for the words I read there
The words were, "Mother is gone"

As I stood alone with memories of home
The place I left long, long ago
I returned home but I waited too long
For the words said, "Mother is gone"

My friends did say before she went away
She called my name o'er and o'er
So trusting in God's love, I'll meet her above
Over on that other shore

Mother is gone to her home
Way up in Heaven above
And my heart's so sad for the words I read there
The words were, "Mother is gone"

Move It On Over

Came in last night at half past ten
That baby of mine wouldn't let me in
     So move it on over,
     Move it on over
Move over little dog 'cause the big dog's movin' in

She changed the lock on our front door
Now my door key don't fit no more
     So get it on over,
     Scoot it on over
Move over skinny dog 'cause the fat dog's movin' in

This doghouse here is mighty small
But it's better than no house at all
     So ease it on over,
     Drag it on over
Move over old dog 'cause the new dog's movin' in

She told me not to play around
But I done let the deal go down
     So pack it on over,
     Tote it on over
Move over nice dog 'cause a bad dog's movin' in

She warned me once, she warned me twice
But I don't take no one's advice
Scratch it on over,
Shake it on over
Move over short dog, 'cause the tall dogs moving in

She'll crawl back to me on her knees
I'll be busy scratchin' fleas
  So slide it on over
  Sneak it on over
Move over good dog, 'cause a mad dog's movin' in

Remember pup before you whine
That side's yours and this side's mine
  So shove it on over
  Sweep it on over
Move over cold dog, 'cause a hot dog's movin' in

My Cold, Cold Heart Is Melted Now

My cold, cold heat is melted now
I seek for peace but don't know how
I go to bed but only weep
My cold, cold heart won't let me sleep

Your lonesome voice that seems to say
"Your cold, cold heart will pay and pay"
My tears pour down like falling rain
Through restless sleep I call your name

Perhaps some day beyond the blue
We'll meet, sweetheart, and live anew
Where cold, cold hearts can't enter in
We'll laugh and love, sweetheart again

My cold, cold heart is melted now
My once proud head I humbly bow
Your lonely face in dreams I see
My cold, cold heart has told on me

My Heart Won't Let Me Go

You don't care one thing about me
And you never will, I know
Still I hang around you darling
You know, I can't let you go

I know you will only hurt me
Just because I love you so
I know I should be leaving
But my heart won't let me go

Tonight, when you are sleeping
I will lie awake and cry
For in my heart I know
That soon you'll say goodbye

How I hate to see tomorrow
It just brings tears and woe
I know I should be leaving
But my heart won't let me go

My Heart Would Know

I could say it's over now
That I was glad to see you go
I could hate you for the way I'm feelin'
My lips could tell a lie
> But my heart would know

It's a sin to make me cry
When you know I love you so
I could tell my heart that I don't miss you
My lips could tell a lie
> But my heart would know

I could give you all the blame
But I'm sure the truth would show
I could tell the world I found a new love
My lips could tell a lie
> But my heart would know

I can't fool my cryin' heart
Cause it knows I need you so
I could tell my heart I'm glad we parted
My lips could tell a lie
> But my heart would know

My Love For You Has Turned To Hate

I'll never forget that sad, sad day
Darling, that you went away
You told me that our love was true
And then you left me alone and blue

Yes, I received your note today
Saying you'd come back and stay
Don't come back now, it is too late
My love for you has turned to hate

Don't come back now on your knees
Tryin' to take me back please
Cause you can't mend my broken heart
Because it died while we were apart

Yes, I received your note today
Saying you'd come back and stay
Don't come back now, it is too late
My love for you has turned to hate

My Son Calls Another Man Daddy

Tonight my head is bowed in sorrow
I can't keep the tears from my eyes
My son calls another man Daddy
The right to his love I've been denied

My son calls another man Daddy
He'll never know my name or my face
God only knows how it hurts me
For another to be in my place

Each night I laid there in prison
I pictured a future so bright
And he was the one ray of sunshine
That shone through the darkness of night

My son calls another man Daddy
He'll never know my name or my face
God only knows how it hurts me
For another to be in my place

Today his mother shares a new love
She just couldn't stand my disgrace
My son calls another man Daddy
And longs for a love he can't replace

My son calls another man Daddy
He'll ne'er know my name or my face
God only knows how it hurts me
For another to be in my place

My Sweet Love Ain't Around

Listen to the rain a-fallin'
Can't you hear that lonesome sound
Oh, my poor old heart is breakin'
Cause my sweet love ain't around

Lord, I think I'll start to ramble
Got to leave this weary town
This old place is way too lonely
Cause my sweet love ain't around

On that train tonight I'm leavin'
And don't ask me where I'm bound
I can't stay here any longer
Cause my sweet love ain't around

Memories come back to haunt me
My dream house has done fell down
This old world is dark around me
Cause my sweet love ain't around

Something tells me that I'm losing
Cause these weary blues I've found
Oh, my baby left this morning
Lord, my sweet love ain't around

'Neath a Cold Gray Tomb of Stone

Standing by a lonesome graveyard
Everything I love is gone
Weeping as they lay my darling
'Neath a cold gray tomb of stone

In this world, I'm left to wander
With no one to call my own
Oh, my precious darling's sleeping
'Neath a cold gray tomb of stone

Out there in that lonesome graveyard
She is sleeping all alone
And they buried my heart with her
'Neath a cold gray tomb of stone

Skies above are dark and stormy
Oh, the sunshine all has flown
And the one I love is sleeping
'Neath a cold gray tomb of stone

My heart's dead and yet I'm living
Wandering through this world alone
I wish that I was with my darling
'Neath that cold gray tomb of stone

Never Again (Will I Knock On Your Door)

Oh you know that I've come back and we've tried it o'er
But each time, my dear, it was worse than before
Now my heart is broke, it's sad and it's sore
So never again will I knock on your door

Oh you know that I love you, no other will do
Please tell me, darling, why can't you be true
But now you are gone, it's over and so
Never again will I knock on your door

Darling, someday you'll be so lonely and blue
Then you will know just how much I love you
But now you are gone, it's over and so
Never again will I knock on your door

Many a night I've cried over you
Hoping and praying some day you'd be true
But now you are gone, it's over I know
So never again will I knock on your door

Oh, you now that I love you, no other will do
Please tell me darling why can't you be true
Now you are gone, it's over and so
Never again will I knock on your door

Never Been So Lonesome

Now the day you left and went away
The mean old blues walked in to stay
I feel like a child without a home
Come back, baby, I'm all alone

I ain't never been so lonesome
In my life before
The day you packed and went away
I never thought that I would say
"I miss you, honey, and I'm lonesome too"
Never thought a soul could be so blue

Ain't been so lonesome in my life before
I need a little lovin', my heart is sick and sore
You left, I don't know why
And if you stay way, I know I'll die
Ain't been so lonesome in my life before

No Not Now

Took my gal to a picture show
Just the other day
But when I tried to hold her hand,
Here's what she had to say
No, not now,
No, not now
No, not now
But maybe next week somehow

Walked my gal home to the door
And asked her for a kiss
But she quickly turned away
And then she told me this
No, not now
No, not now
No, not now
But maybe next week somehow

I asked my gal to marry me,
Reckon what she said
She said, "I wouldn't marry you
If all the rest were dead"
No, not now
No, not now
No, not now
But maybe next week somehow

But she went and changed her mind,
How I regret that day
Cause ever since I married her,
Here's all she can say
No, not now
No, not now
No, not now,
But maybe next week somehow

I stayed out too late last night,
On a little spree,
And when I asked her to let me in,
Here's all she said to me
No, not now
No, not now
No, not now,
But maybe next week somehow

Nobody's Lonesome For Me

Everybody's lonesome for somebody else
But nobody's lonesome for me
Everybody's thinkin' about somebody else
But nobody's thinkin' about me
When the time rolls around for me to lay down and die
I bet I'll have to go and hire me someone to cry
Everybody's lonesome for somebody else
Nobody's lonesome for me

Everybody's longin' for somebody else
But nobody's lonesome for me
Everybody's dreamin' 'bout somebody else
But nobody dreams about me
All I need is a bride who wants a big hearted groom
I wouldn't care if she came ridin' in on a broom
Everybody's lonesome for somebody else
Nobody's lonesome for me

Everybody's pinin' for somebody else
But nobody's lonesome for me
Everybody's crazy 'bout somebody else
But nobody's crazy 'bout me
Oh, I shine up my shoes and then I slick down my hair
Put on my Sunday suit but I ain't goin' nowhere
Everybody's lonesome for somebody else
Nobody's lonesome for me

Everybody's yearnin' for somebody else
But nobody's lonesome for me
Everybody's fallin' for somebody else
But nobody's fallin' for me
Now I ain't had a kiss since I fell out of my crib
It looks to me like I've been cheated out of my rib
Everybody's lonesome for somebody else
Nobody's lonesome for me

Oh, Mama, Come Home

Now I woke up this morning and I looked all 'round
Cause then I realized she'd left this town
Oh mama, come home, oh mama, come home
Oh mama, come home, your daddy is all alone

There's no one now to warm my bed at night
All my days are long and sad and filled with trouble and strife
Oh, Mama, come home, oh, mama, come home
Oh, mama, come home your daddy is all alone

Your daddy is getting worried so blue I can't see
Cooking for these youngin's is slowly killing me
Oh mama, come home, oh mama, come home
Oh mama, come home, your daddy is all alone

But baby, I'm so lonely, nothing going right
Blues they hang around me both day and night
Oh mama, come home, oh mama, come home
Oh mama, come home, your daddy is all alone

Oh mama, come home, oh mama come home
Oh mama, come home, your daddy is all alone
Oh mama, come home, your daddy is all alone
Oh mama, come home, your daddy is all alone

On the Banks of the Old Pontchartrain

I traveled from Texas to old Lousianne,
Through valleys o'er mountains and plain
Both footsore and weary, I rested awhile
     On the banks of the old Pontchartrain

The fairest young maiden that I ever saw
Passed by as it started to rain
We both found a shelter beneath the same tree
     On the banks of the old Pontchartrain

We hid from the shower an hour or so,
She asked me how long I'd remain
I told her that I'd spend the rest of my days
     On the banks of the old Pontchartrain

I just couldn't tell her that I ran away
From jail on a west Texas plain
I prayed in my heart I would never be found
     On the banks of the old Pontchartrain

Then one day a man put his arm on my arm
And said I must go west again
I left alone without saying goodbye
     On the banks of the old Pontchartrain

Tonight as I sit here alone in my cell,

I know that she's waiting in vain

I'm hoping and praying some day to return

    To the banks of the old Pontchartrain

On the Evening Train

The baby's eyes are red from weeping
It's little heart is filled with pain
A Daddy cried, they're taking mama away
      On the evening train

I heard the laughter at the depot
But my tears fell like the rain
When I saw them place that long white casket
In the baggage coach
      Of the evening train

As I turned to walk away from the depot
It seemed I heard her call my name
Take care of baby and tell him, darling, that I'm going home
      On the evening train

I pray that God will give me courage
To carry on till we meet again
It's hard to know she's gone forever
They're carrying her home
      On the evening train

Pan American

I have heard your stories about your fast trains
But now I'll tell you 'bout one all the southern folks have seen
She's the beauty of the southland, listen to that whistle scream
It's that Pan American on her way to New Orleans

She leaves Cincinnati headin' down that Dixie line
When she passed that Nashville tower, you can hear that whistle whine
Stick your head right out the window and feel that southern breeze
You're on that Pan American on her way to New Orleans

If you're ever in the southland and want to see the scenes
Just get yourself a ticket on the Pan American Queen
There's Louisville, Nashville, Montgomery, the capital of Alabam
You pass right through them all when you're New Orleans bound

She leaves Cincinnati headin' down that Dixie line
When she passes that Nashville tower, you can hear that whistle whine
Stick your head right out the window and feel that southern breeze
You're on that Pan American on her way to New Orleans

(I'm Praying For The Day That) Peace Will Come

I am praying for the day
When the whole world can say
That this terrible war is o'er
When the boys who are gone
Start their long journey home
O, I'm praying for the day that peace will come

Recitation:

On behalf of all the people who walk upon this earth, I would
like to say a few words to the leaders of all the great nations of
this world.

Gentlemen, it is within your power today to decide if mankind shall
live in peace or war. It is even within your power to decide if man
shall continue to exist or whether he shall perish from the face of
the earth. Throughout all the world in all nations, men, women and
children are praying that your decisions will lead us into a world of
peace, a world where words such as "hate," "fear" and "aggression"
will be replaced by "love," "peace" and "understanding."

Is it not better to lift up your hearts to your God than to lift your
eyes to a heaven filled with atomic bombs? The decisions are
yours, but we the people of the world will bear the consequence
of your decisions. Someone said, and I'm sure it is true, whatever
man can think of man can achieve. May you humbly and
honestly think in terms of peace, as for myself...

I am praying for the day
When the whole world can say
That this terrible war is o'er
When the boys who are gone
Start their long journey home
O, I'm praying for the day that peace will come

A Picture From Life's Other Side

In the world's mighty gallery of pictures
Hang the scenes that are painted from life
There's pictures of love and passion
There's pictures of peace and of strife

There hang pictures of youth and of beauty
Of old age and a blushing young bride
  They all hung on the wall
  But the saddest of all
Are the pictures from life's other side

Just a picture from life's other side
Someone has fell by the way
A life has gone out with the tide
That might have been happy some day

There's a poor old mother at home
She's watching and waiting alone
  Just longing to hear
  From a loved one so dear
Just a picture from life's other side

The first scene is that of a gambler
Who had lost all of his money at play
And he draws his dead mother's ring from his finger
That she wore long ago on her wedding day

It's his last earthly treasure but he stakes it
Then he bows his head that his shame he might hide
  But when they lifted his head,
  They found he was dead
That's just a picture from life's other side

Now the last scene is that by the river
Of a heartbroken mother and babe
As the harbor lights shine and they shiver
On an outcast whom no one will save

And yet she was once a true woman
She was somebody's darling and pride
  God help her, she leaps,
  But there's no one to weep
It's just a picture from life's other side

Please Make Up Your Mind

When I agree with you, baby, it makes you mad
And when I don't, it makes you sad
When I argue back you pack and leave
And when I don't you pout and grieve
There just ain't nobody knows what I go through
Will you please make up your mind what you want me to do?

You say "Get out" and I'd better stay gone
Then you have a big policeman drag me back home
You hollar good and loud "Put him in the calaboose"
Then you cry and ask the judge, "Won't you please turn him loose"
The good Lord knows what I go through
Will you please make up your mind what you want me to do?

My life with you has been one hard knock
Lord, my head looks like an old chop block
And I'll tell you right now, honey, that ain't all
You done kicked me till I feel like a used football
There just ain't nobody knows what I go through
Will you please make up your mind what you want me to do?

You knock me down and then you pick me up
Honey, do you have to love so doggone rough
I wish to my soul you'd slow down the pace
Cause I tell you right now, the hide's gettin' sc'ace
There just ain't nobody knows what I go through
Will you please make up your mind what you want me to do?

Why, when I married you, you were such a meek little thing
But, honey, among tigers, you'd be queen
If a poor little rabbit had you on his side
Every hound in the country would crawl off and hide
There just ain't nobody knows what I go through
Will you please make up your mind what you want me to do?

What in the confounded cat hair do you want me to do?

Ramblin' Man

I can settle down and be doin' just fine
'Til I hear an old freight rollin' down the line
Then I hurry straight home and pack
And if I didn't go, I believe I'd blow my stack
I love you baby, but you gotta understand
When the Lord made me, He made a ramblin' man

Some folks might say that I'm no good
That I wouldn't settle down if I could
But when that open road starts to callin' me
There's something o'er the hill that I gotta see
Sometimes it's hard, but you gotta understand
When the Lord made me, He made a ramblin' man

I love to see the towns a-passin' by
And to ride these rails 'neath God's blue sky
Let me travel this land from the mountains to the sea
Cause that's the life I believe He meant for me
And when I'm gone and at my grave you stand
Just say God's called home your ramblin' man

Ready To Go Home

There's coming a day
When the world shall melt away
And Jesus shall come to claim His own
No more tears, no pain,
No woe in this wicked world below
Then will you be ready to go home?

Will you be ready,
      Ready to go home?
To live with Him
      Up there 'round the throne?
When He says, "Come unto Me,"
Will our soul be clean and free?
Then will you be ready to go home?

In this world of greed and hate,
Will you wait till it's too late,
Too late to claim the Savior for you own?
For He's coming someday
To bear your soul away
Then will you be ready to go home?

Will you be ready,
      Ready to go home?
To live with Him
      Up there 'round the throne?

When He says, "Come unto Me,"
Will our soul be clean and free?
Then will you be ready to go home?

As you travel day by day
Down life's long highway
Are you on the road that leads to wrong?
If you'll just travel in His light
And pray both day and night
Then you'll be ready to go home

Rockin' Chair Daddy

I'm not lazy, I'm just tired
I get me a job and I get fired
Not scared of work, but it makes me weak
I can lay down beside it and fall off sound asleep

I'm a rockin' chair daddy from Tennessee
And the woman I marry, she's sure got to wait on me
She's got to boil my coffee and strain my tea
Cause I'm a rockin' chair daddy
      From way down in Tennessee

No more jobs left on this earth
People only pay for what you're worth
Cause there ain't no use of me workin' so hard
Cause I ain't even got me a Union card

I'm a rockin' chair daddy from Tennessee
And the woman I marry, she's sure got to wait on me
She's got to boil my coffee and strain my tea
Cause I'm a rockin' chair daddy
      From way down in Tennessee

I want my biscuits brown and my ham well done
My shirts bleached white in the noonday sun
When I want something, I want it now
Then that woman of mine could kiss me on the brow

I'm a rockin' chair daddy from Tennessee
And the woman I marry, she's sure got to wait on me
She's got to boil my coffee and strain my tea
Cause I'm a rockin' chair daddy
     From way down in Tennessee

The Sermon on the Mount

A man sat on a mountainside, a carpenter by trade
Teaching His disciples while they knelt and prayed
He blessed the poor and simple and He brought the mourners joy
He came to heal the blind and lame they came not to destroy

When smitten by His enemies, He turned the other cheek
He brought strength of God and morals to mortals who were weak
He told of false prophets who wore a sheep's disguise
And He warned us not to trust him or to listen to his lies

Hey, the sermon on the mountainside will live eternally
He'll lead us to the kingdom and He'll promise you and me
So take the straight and narrow and do good things that count
Make up your mind to live by the sermon on the mount

Singing Waterfall

There's a singing waterfall
In the mountains far away
There's where I long to be
At the close of every day
There's where my sweetheart's sleeping
Down beneath the clay
I often sit and wonder
Why the Lord took her away

We met there every evenin'
When the sun was sinkin' low
And we'd listen to the waters
As they rippled soft and low
And since she's gone to Heaven,
I miss her most of all
Tonight my darlin's sleeping
By the singin' waterfall

Last night as I lay dreaming,
I heard my darlin' call
And then I went to meet her
By the singin' waterfall
She took me in her arms,
Just like she used to do
And then I heard her whisper
We'll meet beyond the blue

Six More Miles

Oh the rain is slowly fallin'
And my heart is so sore
Six more miles and leave my darlin'
Never on this earth to meet no more

Six more miles to the graveyard
Six more miles long and sad
Six more miles and leave my darlin'
Leave the best friend I ever had

Oh I heard the train a-coming
Bringing my darlin' back home
Six more miles to the graveyard
And I'll be left here all alone

Six more miles to the graveyard
Six more miles long and sad
Six more miles and leave my darlin'
Leave the best friend I ever had

Six more miles to the graveyard
Six more miles long and sad
Six more miles and leave my darlin'
Leave the best friend I ever had

Somebody's Lonesome

Somebody's heart is breaking tonight
Somebody's lost on life's sea
Somebody's paying for being untrue
Somebody's lonesome, and that somebody's me

Somebody's life is now filled with tears
And their heart will never be free
Doomed to a life, to pay and regret
Somebody's lonesome, and somebody's me

Somebody's lied to a heart that was true
And somebody must pay the fee
Somebody now, is crying in vain
Somebody's lonesome, and that somebody's me

Somebody now, would gladly give his life
To bring back the sweet used-to-be
And try to repay all the wrong he has done
Somebody's lonesome, and that somebody's me

A Stranger in the Night

I'm lonesome for someone to kiss me goodnight
      Just the way you used to do
My achin' heart needs someone to shine love's light
      For without you I'll always be blue

If I don't have you to help me along
      I know I can never go right
Without you beside me to show the way
      I'm lost like a stranger in the night

Like a lonely dove that flies from pine to pine
      My heart can't be gay and light
Like sightless eyes that will never see the sun
      I'm lost like a stranger in the night

There's no need for me to even try
      Nothing will ever turn out right
When I lost your love, I lost the will to live
      And I'm lost like a stranger in the night

Like a broken heart, that's lost on life's sea,
Though I pray with all my might,
I know I can't face, tomorrow alone
And I'm lost like a stranger in the night

A Teardrop on a Rose

While strolling through a lovely garden
As day was drawing to a close
My eyes beheld a tragic story
I saw a teardrop on a rose

It should have been a tear of gladness
But deep inside the sorrow showed
A trusting heart had just been broken
I saw a teardrop on a rose

A sobbing tear that follows parting
Holds all the pain that sorrow knows
A false goodbye, a life is shattered
There lies a story on a rose

The tear will dry, the rose will wither
When Spring and Winter comes and goes
I loved, I lost, my story ended
With just a teardrop on a rose

There'll Be No Teardrops Tonight

I'll pretend I'm free from sorrow
Make believe that wrong is right
Your wedding day will be tomorrow
But there'll be no teardrops tonight

Why, oh why, should you desert me
Are you doing this for spite
If you only want to hurt me
Then there'll be no teardrops tonight

I'll believe that you still love me
When you wear your veil of white
But you think that you're above me
But there'll be no teardrops tonight

Shame, oh shame, for what you're doing
Other arms will hold you tight
You don't care whose life you ruin
But there'll be no teardrops tonight

There's a Tear in My Beer

There's a tear in my beer,
Cause I'm crying for you, dear
You are on my lonely mind

Into these last nine beers
I have shed a million tears
You are on my lonely mind

I'm gonna keep drinkin'
Until I'm petrified
And then maybe these tears will leave my eyes

There's a tear in my beer
Cause I'm cryin' for you, dear
You are on my lonely mind

Last night I walked the floor
And the night before
You are on my lonely mind

It seems my life is through
And I'm so doggone blue
You are on my lonely mind

I'm gonna keep on drinkin' here
Till I can't move a toe
And then maybe my heart won't hurt so

There's a tear in my beer
Cause I'm crying for you, dear
You are on my lonely mind

Lord, I've tried and I've tried
But my tears I can't hide
You are on my lonely mind.

All these blues that I've found
Have really got me down
You are on my lonely mind

I'm gonna keep drinkin' till I can't even think
Cause in the last week I ain't slept a wink

There's a tear in my beer
Cause I'm crying for you, dear
You are on my lonely mind.

There's Nothing As Sweet As My Baby

I like candy, I like cake
I like jam but goodness sake,
There's nothing as sweet as my baby

Golden hair and big blue eyes
She could win a beauty prize
There's nothing as sweet as my baby

If I ever lose her, I'll lay me down and die
If sugar seems sweet then you ought to meet
      My honey coated sweetie pie

I like candy, I like cake
I like jam but goodness sake
There's nothing as sweet as my baby

I feel like a honey bee
When she's buzzin' around with me
There's nothing as sweet as my baby

Get pounds of candy kisses, but I can't spare an ounce
She's sweeter than wine, and brother, she's mine
      And that's the only thing that counts

I like candy, I like cake
I like jam but goodness sake
There's nothing as sweet as my baby

Time Has Proven I Was Wrong

There was a time I thought you loved me
And that we two could get along
But now I know I was just dreaming
For time has proven I was wrong

I built a world for us together
But love to you was just a song
And now I know I was mistaken
For time has proven I was wrong

We're Getting Closer to the Grave Each Day

Oh, don't you know that Jesus died
To wash your sins away
      Please heed His call
      And in sin don't fall
We're getting closer to the grave each day

Mortal man, won't you stop and pray
Leave the road of sin alone,
Let Jesus lead you home
We're getting closer to the grave each day

They nailed His hands, they pierced His sides
On His head the thorns did lay
      Be prepared to go,
      There's one thing I know
We're getting closer to the grave each day

We're getting closer to the grave each day
Sinner man, won't you stop now and pray
      Leave the road of sin alone,
      Let Jesus lead you home
We're getting closer to the grave each day

On the judgment day when life's book is read
There'll be no time to pray
      Learn to love and forgive
      While on earth you live
We're getting closer to the grave each day

Wealth Won't Save Your Soul

As we journey along on life's wicked road
So selfish are we for silver and gold
You can treasure your wealth, your diamonds and gold
But my friends it won't save your poor wicked soul

For when God calls from His home up on high
To your earthly wealth you must say good-bye
Then it's useless to you if you've strayed from the fold
For my friend it won't save your poor wicked soul

The rich man like Paul will be judged at that time
But all of his wealth will be left behind
For no matter how much earthly wealth you dear hold
My friends it won't save your poor wicked soul

Wearin' Out Your Walkin' Shoes

Well, you can't live with 'em,
You can't live without 'em
Yet there's somethin'
Mighty necessary 'bout 'em
A woman will give you the blues
    She'll have you pullin' out your hair,
    And wearin' out your walkin' shoes

Well, they just keep naggin'
Until your head is saggin'
There ain't a wink of sleepin'
When they start weepin'
Cause a woman will give you the blues
    She'll have you bitin' off your nails
    And wearin' out your walkin' shoes

It's a losin' gamble
When you start to ramble
Oh, Lordy, how you miss 'em
And you long to kiss 'em
Cause a woman will give you the blues
    She'll have you tossin' in your sleep
    And wearin' out your walkin' shoes

Well, you can't live with 'em,
You can't live without 'em
It's better to talk with 'em
Than to talk about 'em
Cause a woman will give you the blues
     She'll have you talkin' to yourself
     And wearin' out your walkin' shoes

Weary Blues from Waiting

Weary blues from waitin'
Lord, I've been waitin' too long
These blues have got me cryin'
Oh, sweet Mama, please come home

The snow falls round my window
But it can't chill my heart
God knows it died the day you left
My dream world fell apart

Weary blues from waitin'
Lord, I've been waitin' too long
These blues have got me cryin'
Oh, sweet Mama, please come home

Through tears I watch young lovers
As they go strollin' by
Oh, all the things that might have been
God forgive me if I cry

Weary blues from waitin'
Lord, I've been waitin' too long
These blues have got me cryin'
Oh, sweet Mama, please come home

When God Comes and Gathers His Jewels

The ceremony was over,
A lad stood alone in tears
For he had just said good-bye
To the one he had loved through the years
He stood all alone with his head bowed down
　　　As though his heart would break
The parson came over and took his hand
　　　And to him these words he did say

When God comes and gather His jewels
All His treasure of diamonds and gold
　　　You'll meet her up there
　　　Up in Heaven so fair
When God comes and gathers His jewels

Each night when the pale moon is shining
You can see this lad all alone
With his eyes lifted toward Heaven
He's repeating these words he was told

When God comes and gather His jewels
All His treasure of diamonds and gold
　　　I'll meet you up there
　　　Up in Heaven so fair
When God comes and gathers His jewels

When the Book of Life is Read

In life's many battles
That you will have to fight
Just stay close to Jesus
And journey in His light
Then on that Judgment Morning
When all pain has fled
You'll stand in God's Kingdom
     When the Book of Life is read

When the seals are broken
And names are read aloud
You'll see many loved ones
Standing in the crowd
So, brother, keep on praying
And follow where you're led
You'll stand in God's Kingdom
     When the Book of Life is read

All your dreams of Heaven
Will come true on that day
When the sky shall open
And this earth melt away
Then all God's faithful children
Will raise up from the dead
United in God's Kingdom
     When the Book of Life is read

What a happy feeling
To know He'll always care
And when our work is over,
Heaven with Him we'll share
There'll be no pain or sorrow,
No tears will o'er be shed
When we stand there in God's Kingdom
    And the Book of Life is read

When You're Tired of Breaking Other Hearts

When you're tired of breaking other hearts
    Won't you come back again and break mine
When you're tired of roaming, Darling
    And the love light no longer shines
When your dream world falls around you
    And you sit by yourself and pine
When you're tired of breaking other hearts
    Won't you come back again and break mine

Where Do I Go From Here

Slowly but surely I've watched your love die
And now you run my heart over with care
I know, oh so well, that you don't want me now
Tell me, darling, where do I go from here?

I've built all my plans and hopes around you
And no other could replace you, dear
I've seen all my dreams and my hopes fade away
Tell me darling, where do I go from here?

You know that your pride is making you stay
But sympathy ain't what I want to hear
And what good is kindness to a man that needs love
So tell me, darling, where do I go from here?

I know that your heart is far away
And there's nothing for me but my tears
I didn't want to see my tears turn to hate
So, my darling, I'm going from here

Why Don't You Love Me

Well, why don't you love me like you used to do?
How come you treat me like a worn out shoe
My hair's still curly and my eyes are still blue,
Why don't you love me like you used to do?

Ain't had no lovin', like a-huggin' and a-kissin'
In a long, long while
We don't get nearer or further or closer than a country mile

Why don't you spark me like you used to do?
And say sweet nothings like you used to coo?
I'm the same old trouble that you've always been through,
So why don't you love me like you used to do?

Well, why don't you be just like you used to be?
How come you find so many faults with me?
Somebody's changed, so let me give you a clue,
Why don't you love me like you used to do?

Ain't had no lovin', like a-huggin' and a kissin'
In a long, long while.
We don't get nearer or further or closer than country mile.

Why don't you say the things you used to say?
What makes you treat me like a piece of clay?
My hair's still curly and my eyes are still blue,
Why don't you love me like you used to do?

Why Don't You Make Up Your Mind

When I agree with you, baby it makes you mad
And when I don't, it makes you sad
When I argue back you pack and leave
And when I don't, you pout in grieve
There just ain't nobody knows what I go through
Will you please make up your mind what you want me to do?

You say get out and I'd better stay gone
Then you have a big policeman drag me back home
You holler good and loud, Put him in the calaboose
Then you cry and ask the judge, Won't you please turn him loose
The good Lord only knows what I go through
Will you please make up your mind what you want me to do?

My life with you has been one hard knock
Lord, my head looks like an old chop block
And I'll tell you right now, honey, that ain't all
You done kicked me till I feel like a used football
There just ain't nobody knows what I go through
Will you please make up your mind what you want me to do?
You knock me down and then you pick me up
Honey, do you have to love so doggone rough?
I wish to my soul you'd slow down the pace
Cause I tell you right now the hide's getting scarce
There just ain't nobody knows what I go through
Will you please make up your mind what you want me to do?

Why when I married you, you were such a meek little thing
But honey, among tigers you'd be queen
If a poor little rabbit had you on his side
Every hound in the country would crawl off and hide
There just ain't nobody knows what I go through
Will you please make up your mind
What in the confounded cat hair do you want me to do?

Why Should I Cry

Why should I cry,
I've never done you wrong
I kept my vows,
You left me all alone
You told me you loved me,
You told me a lie
Why should I pay,
Tell me why should I cry?

You know I worshipped you
Right from the start
Gave you my love,
Never thought that we'd part
You didn't care enough
To even say good-bye
Why should I pay,
Tell me why should I cry?

You know I miss you
Now that you've gone
Life can be sad
When you're living alone
But, darling, I'll forget you,
Your memory will die
Why should I pay,
Why should I cry?

Why Should We Try Anymore

What's the use to deny
We've been living a lie
That we should have admitted before
We were just victims
Of a half-hearted love
So why should we try anymore?

The vows that we make
Are only to break
We drift like a wave from the shore
The kisses we steal
We know are not real
So why should we try anymore?

The dreams that we knew
Can never come true
They're gone to return no more
False love like ours
Fades with the flowers
So why should we try anymore?

Our story's so old
Again has been told
On the past let's close the door.
And smile, don't regret,
But live and forget
There's no use to try anymore.

Won't You Sometimes Think of Me

Though our paths in life have parted
You no longer care for me
But when you're happy with another
Won't you sometimes think of me?

When the evenin' sun is sinking
Down behind the trees
And the moon is slowly rising
Won't you sometimes think of me?

I'll always keep your picture
It means so much to me
And every night I'll pray dear
That you'll sometimes think of me

Think of days that are gone dear
Days we could recall
If you would only try dear
But still you blame me for all

When the evenin' sun is sinking
Down behind the trees
And the moon is slowly rising
Won't you sometimes think of me?

All I can say is I tried dear
But you wouldn't let it be

So if you're ever sad and lonely
Won't you sometimes think of me?

When the evening sun is sinking
Down behind the trees
And the moon is slowly rising
Won't you sometimes think of me?

You Better Keep It On Your Mind

Now, if you go out and start to playin' around
Your baby's gonna tear your playhouse down
You better keep it on your mind (all the time)
You better keep it on your mind (all the time)
     You'll be moanin' and a-groanin'
Lawd, you better keep it on your mind

Now, wrong is wrong and right is right
If you make a snake mad, he's sure gonna bite
You better keep it on your mind (all the time)
You better keep it on your mind (all the time)
     I've had it proven to me
Lawd, you better keep it on your mind

Every fuss with a woman's got the same old end
I don't believe the good Lord meant for a man to win
You better keep it on your mind (all the time)
You better keep it on your mind (all the time)
     You'll be singing' low and lonesome
Lawd, you better keep it on your mind

If you make your baby mad and she says, "Goodbye"
There ain't a thing you can do but sit at home and cry
You better keep it on your mind (all the time)
You better keep it on your mind (all the time)
     You better call her "Sweet Mama"

Lawd, you better keep it on your mind
If the judge says "Pay her forty dollars a week"
You'll dig up the money or you'll work the street
You better keep it on your mind (all the time)
You better keep it on your mind (all the time)
      When you're wearin' striped breeches
Son, it's gonna stay on your mind

So, kiss her every mornin' and love her every night
Boy, you can't win, no matter if you're right
You better keep it on your mind (all the time)
You better keep it on your mind (all the time)
      You better heed this warnin'
Lawd, you better keep it on your mind

You Broke Your Own Heart

Your letter says you're unhappy
Since we're many miles apart
It's a little late to ask for pity
You broke your own heart

You walked on the heart that loved you
Had no pity from the start
    You cheated and lied
    And now you're gonna cry
Remember, you broke your own heart

A heart can stand so much sorrow
And then it bends and breaks
And a love that is honest and true
Can turn to bitter hate

Now that you're gone and lonely
And your dreams have fallen apart
Think of the one that once loved you
Remember, you broke your own heart

You Can't Take My Memories of You

Today, you tell me you are leaving
That you are going far away
Darling, I have no way of holding you
So this is all that I can say

You can't take my memories of you
You can go and leave me, oh, so blue
You can break my heart and you can make me cry
But you can't take my memories of you

I tried every way to make you happy
But I guess it was never meant to be
So, today you say you are going
Far away across the deep blue sea

Now after you are gone my darling
Each night I go down to the sea
And gaze at the stars as I wonder where you are
And pray some day that you'll come back to me
But you can't take my memories

You Know That I Know

Now you know that I know
That you ain't no good
And you wouldn't tell the truth even if you could
Lying is a habit you practice wherever you go
Well, you may fool the rest of this world
But you know that I know

Now you told some of my friends
That you'd turn me down
But I wouldn't take you if you're the last gal in town
If I had wanted you, I could've got you long ago
Well, you may fool the rest of this world
But you know that I know

So, baby, when you pass me
Don't you give me the run-around
Cause if you recall correctly
I'm the guy that brought you to town

To some folks you may be Mrs. So-and-So
But don't turn your nose up at me
Cause you know that I know

The last time I saw you, your pretty hair was red
But today I see you've got black hair on your head
You say you've got you a new man with plenty of dough
But, baby, you may fool him

But you know that I know
So, baby, when you pass me
Don't you give me the run-around
Cause if you recall correctly
I'm the man that brought you to town

To some folks you may be Mrs. So-and-So
But, baby, you may fool them
But you know that I know
Yes, you may fool the rest of this world
But you know that I know

You Win Again

The news is out all over town
That you've been seen a-runnin' round
I know that I should leave, but then,
I just can't go, you win again

You have no heart, you have no shame
You take true love and give the blame
I guess that I should not complain
I love you still, you win again

I'm sorry for your victim now
Cause soon his head, like mine, will bow
He'll give his heart, but all in vain
And someday say, you win again

This heart of mine could never see
What everybody knew but me
Just trusting you was my great sin
What can I do, you win again.

You'll Never Again Be Mine

I'm living with a-days that forever are gone
And a heart that does a-nothing but pine
To love and to want you, I know it's wrong
When you'll never again be mine
No, you'll never again be mine

To worship you, darling, the way that I do
I know is just a-wasting my time
Yet my foolish heart cries each day for you
No, you'll never again be mine
No, you'll never again be mine

My lonely heart holds no hatred or pain
Though sometimes I feel it may die
But it always beats stronger
When I hear your name
And it won't let me say goodbye

I tell my heart to live and forget
Someday a new love it will find
But each day it lives is filled with regret
When you'll never again be mine
No, you'll never again be mine

You're Barkin' Up the Wrong Tree Now

You're barkin' up the wrong tree now
You're barkin' up the wrong tree now
    You don't ever want to play
    Unless you have your way
You're barkin' up the wrong tree now

Two can play that cheatin' game
Just as good as one
And I'm the person that can show you how
    If you think I'm second rate
    Then you're gonna lose some weight
Cause you're barkin' up the wrong tree now

You're barkin' up the wrong tree now
You're barkin' up the wrong tree now
    When you get dissatisfied
    Let your conscience be your guide
Cause you're barkin' up the wrong tree now

Two can play that cheatin' game
Just as good as one
And I'm the person that can show you how
    If you want to chase about
    Just don't let me find it out
Cause you're barkin' up the wrong tree now

You're barkin' up the wrong tree now
You're barkin' up the wrong tree now
      Just be sure you never do
      What you don't want done to you
Cause you're barkin' up the wrong tree now

Two can play that cheatin' game
just as good as one
and I'm the person that can show you how
      If it's time you want to spend
      Then you're on the losin' end
Cause you're barkin' up the wrong tree now

You're Gonna Change (Or I'm Gonna Leave)

You wore out a brand new trunk
Packin' and unpackin' your junk
Your Daddy's mad, he's done got peeved
You're gonna change or I'm gonna leave

You're gonna change your way of livin'
Change the things you do
Stop doin' all the things
That you oughtn't to
Your daddy's mad, he's done got peeved
You're gonna change, or I'm gonna leave

This ain't right, that is wrong
You just keep naggin'
All the day long
It's gotta stop, I don't mean please
You're gonna change or I'm gonna leave

The way to keep a woman happy
Make her do what's right
Is love her every mornin'
Bawl her out at night
Your Daddy's mad, He's done got peeved
You're gonna change or I'm gonna leave

Every time that you get mad
You pack your rags and go back to Dad
You tell him lies he don't believe
You're gonna change or I'm gonna leave

You're gonna change your way of livin',
Change the things you do
Stop doin' all the things
That you oughtn't to
Your Daddy's mad, he's done got peeved
You're gonna change, or I'm gonna leave

You're Through Fooling Me

I know someday I'll forget you
Until that day I'll be sober
Go and have your fun
Cause baby, this race is run

You ain't the kind that can be true
You lie and cheat in all that you do
You're through fooling me
Cause I'm through fooling with you

Oh, love this true can turn to hate
You are the cause, don't blame it on fate
You're through fooling me
Cause I'm through fooling with you

I ain't got time to nurse a broke heart
You go stiff and I'll do my part
I'll go stiffing too, it ain't hard to do

I'll find a love that can be true
You find that you're sad and sober
You're through fooling me
Cause I'm through fooling with you

Oh, love this true can turn to hate
You are the cause, don't blame it on fate
You're through fooling me
Cause I'm through fooling with you

Oh, you're through fooling me
Cause I'm through fooling with you

You've Been Lonesome Too

If your heart has known such pain
Until for death it's crying
Only to have the Lord refuse
Then you've been near my side

If in your heart somehow you know
You'll fail whatever you do
Then you have walked a road of pain
Yes, you've been lonesome too

If you have had each joy of life
Destroyed and cast away
Then watch a heart that once knew love
Grow sadder day by day

If your soul is wilted like a rose
That's never felt the dew
You're traveling on the street of grief
Yes, you've been lonesome too

If for your wasted wicked life
Your soul cries out in shame
And you could live it all again
It'd never be the same

If you've cried "God, please bless the one
To whom I was untrue"
You've lived the life of regret
Yes, you've been lonesome too

If when the storms light up the skies
It seems you can't go on
Then from a vision your darling comes
You speak but she is gone

If then the tears flood down your cheeks
There's no one else for you
Then you can't ever hide from fate
Yes, you've been lonesome too

Your Cheatin' Heart

Your cheatin' heart will make you weep
You'll cry and cry and try to sleep
But sleep won't come the whole night through
Your cheatin' heart will tell on you

When tears come down, like fallin' rain
You'll toss around and call my name
You'll walk the floor the way I do
Your cheatin' heart will tell on you

Your cheatin' heart will pine someday
And crave the love you threw away
The time will come when you'll be blue
Your cheatin' heart will tell on you

When tears come down, like fallin' rain
You'll toss around and call my name
You'll walk the floor the way I do
Your cheatin' heart will tell on you

Your Turn To Cry

The day that we parted
You laughed when I cried
You said you didn't care
That your love had died
Now you say you're sorry
That you said good-bye
Now it's my turn to laugh
      And your turn to cry

Darling, when you left me
I thought my life was through
Everything that I did reminded me of you
But now I've forgotten,
No more tears in my eyes
It's my turn to laugh
      And your turn to cry

My turn to laugh,
Your turn to cry
My love was true,
Your's was a lie
But now I've forgotten,
No more tears in my eyes
Now it's my turn to laugh
      And your turn to cry

Hank Williams
Copyright Permissions
Hank Williams Copyright Notices

ARE YOU LONELY TOO
CAJUN BABY
FOR ME THERE IS NO PLACE
HOMESICK
I'M JUST CRYING 'CAUSE I CARE
IS THIS GOODBYE
JUST ME AND MY BROKEN HEART
MY HEART WON'T LET ME GO
SOMEBODY'S LONESOME
WHERE DO I GO FROM HERE
YOU BROKE YOUR OWN HEART
YOU CAN'T TAKE MY MEMORIES OF YOU
YOUR TURN TO CRY

I'M SO TIRED OF IT ALL

BAYOU PON PON
FOREVER'S A LONG LONG TIME
50% Hank Williams Sr. (BMI) – Sony/ATV Acuff Rose Music (BMI)
50% Jimmie Davis (BMI) – Sony/ATV Acuff Rose Music (BMI)

© 1951 Sony/ATV Music Publishing LLC.
All rights administered by Sony/ATV Music Publishing LLC.
424 Church Street, Suite 1200, Nashville, TN 37219. All rights
reserved. Used by permission.

HONEY DO YOU LOVE ME HUH
50% Hank Williams Sr. (BMI) – Sony/ATV Acuff Rose Music (BMI)
50% Curley Williams (BMI) – Sony/ATV Acuff Rose Music (BMI)

© 1950 Sony/ATV Music Publishing LLC.
All rights administered by Sony/ATV Music Publishing LLC.
424 Church Street, Suite 1200, Nashville, TN 37219. All rights
reserved. Used by permission.

I LOST THE ONLY LOVE I KNEW
50% Hank Williams Sr. (BMI) – Sony/ATV Acuff Rose Music (BMI)
50% Don Helms (BMI) – Sony/ATV Acuff Rose Music (BMI)

© 1952 Sony/ATV Music Publishing LLC.
All rights administered by Sony/ATV Music Publishing LLC.
424 Church Street, Suite 1200, Nashville, TN 37219. All rights
reserved. Used by permission.

I'LL NEVER GET OUT OF THIS WORLD ALIVE
50% Hank Williams Sr. (BMI) – Sony/ATV Milene Music (ASCAP)
50% Fred Rose (ASCAP) – Sony/ATV Milene Music (ASCAP)
© 1952 Sony/ATV Music Publishing LLC.

IF I DIDN'T LOVE YOU
MANSION ON THE HILL
50% Hank Williams Sr. (BMI) – Sony/ATV Milene Music (ASCAP)
50% Fred Rose (ASCAP) – Sony/ATV Milene Music (ASCAP)

I HOPE YOU SHED A MILLION TEARS
50% Hank Williams Sr. (BMI) – Sony/ATV Acuff Rose Music (BMI)
6.25% Rodney Crowell (ASCAP) – Sony/ATV Milene Music (ASCAP)

JESUS IS CALLING
50% Hank Williams Sr. (BMI) – Sony/ATV Acuff Rose Music (BMI)
50% Charlie Monroe (BMI) – Sony/ATV Acuff Rose Music (BMI)

YOU'VE BEEN LONESOME TOO

50% Hank Williams Sr. (BMI) – Sony/ATV Acuff Rose Music (BMI)
50% Alan Jackson (ASCAP) – EMI April Music Inc. (45%) / Tri-Angels Music (5%) (ASCAP)

© 2001 Sony/ATV Music Publishing LLC., EMI April Music Inc., & Tri-Angels Music
All rights administered by Sony/ATV Music Publishing LLC. 424 Church Street, Suite 1200, Nashville, TN 37219. All rights reserved. Used by permission.

YOU'RE BARKING UP THE WRONG TREE NOW

50% Hank Williams Sr. (BMI) – Sony/ATV Milene Music (ASCAP)
50% Fred Rose (ASCAP) – Sony/ATV Milene Music (ASCAP)

© 1949 Sony/ATV Music Publishing LLC.
All rights administered by Sony/ATV Music Publishing LLC. 424 Church Street, Suite 1200, Nashville, TN 37219. All rights reserved. Used by permission.

YOU BETTER KEEP IT ON YOUR MIND

50% Hank Williams Sr. (BMI) – Sony/ATV Acuff Rose Music (BMI)
50% Vic Mcalpin (BMI) – Sony/ATV Acuff Rose Music (BMI)

© 1954 Sony/ATV Music Publishing LLC.
All rights administered by Sony/ATV Music Publishing LLC. 424 Church Street, Suite 1200, Nashville, TN 37219. All rights reserved. Used by permission.

WHEN YOU'RE TIRED OF BREAKING OTHER HEARTS

50% Hank Williams Sr. (BMI) – Sony/ATV Acuff Rose Music (BMI)
50% Curley Williams (BMI) – Sony/ATV Acuff Rose Music (BMI)

A STRANGER IN THE NIGHT

50% Hank Williams Sr. (BMI) – Sony/ATV Acuff Rose Music (BMI)
50% Bill Morgan (BMI) – Sony/ATV Acuff Rose Music (BMI)

TIME HAS PROVEN I WAS WRONG

33.33% Hank Williams Sr. (BMI) – Sony/ATV Acuff Rose Music (BMI)
33.34% Curley Williams (BMI) – Sony/ATV Acuff Rose Music (BMI)
33.33% Mel Foree (BMI) – Sony/ATV Acuff Rose Music (BMI)

JUST WAITIN'

50% Hank Williams Sr. (BMI) – Sony/ATV Acuff Rose Music (BMI)
50% Bob Gazzaway (BMI) – Sony/ATV Acuff Rose Music (BMI)

KAW LIGA
50% Hank Williams Sr. (BMI) – Sony/ATV Milene Music (ASCAP)
50% Fred Rose (ASCAP) – Sony/ATV Milene Music (ASCAP)

© 1952 Sony/ATV Music Publishing LLC.
All rights administered by Sony/ATV Music Publishing LLC.
424 Church Street, Suite 1200, Nashville, TN 37219. All rights
reserved. Used by permission.

LITTLE HOUSE WE BUILT (JUST O'ER THE HILL), THE
50% Hank Williams Sr. (BMI) – Sony/ATV Acuff Rose Music (BMI)
50% Don Helms (BMI) – Sony/ATV Acuff Rose Music (BMI)

© 1951 Sony/ATV Music Publishing LLC.
All rights administered by Sony/ATV Music Publishing LLC.
424 Church Street, Suite 1200, Nashville, TN 37219. All rights
reserved. Used by permission.

MY COLD HEART IS MELTED NOW
50% Hank Williams Sr. (BMI) – Sony/ATV Acuff Rose Music (BMI)
50% Johnnie Masters (BMI) – Sony/ATV Acuff Rose Music (BMI)

© 1953 Sony/ATV Music Publishing LLC.
All rights administered by Sony/ATV Music Publishing LLC.
424 Church Street, Suite 1200, Nashville, TN 37219. All rights
reserved. Used by permission.

MY SON CALLS ANOTHER MAN DADDY
50% Hank Williams Sr. (BMI) – Sony/ATV Acuff Rose Music (BMI)
50% Jewell House (BMI) – Sony/ATV Acuff Rose Music (BMI)

ON THE BANKS OF THE OLD PONTCHARTRAIN
50% Hank Williams Sr. (BMI) – Sony/ATV Acuff Rose Music (BMI)
50% Ramona Vincent (BMI) – Sony/ATV Acuff Rose Music (BMI)

ON THE EVENING TRAIN
50% Hank Williams Sr. (BMI) – Sony/ATV Acuff Rose Music (BMI)
50% Audrey Williams (BMI) – Sony/ATV Acuff Rose Music (BMI)

ROCKIN' CHAIR DADDY
50% Hank Williams Sr. (BMI) – Sony/ATV Acuff Rose Music (BMI)
50% Braxton Shooford (BMI) – Sony/ATV Acuff Rose Music (BMI)

NO NOT NOW

33.33% Hank Williams Sr. (BMI) – Sony/ATV Acuff Rose Music (BMI)

33.33% Curley Williams (BMI) – Sony/ATV Acuff Rose Music (BMI)

33.34% Mel Foree (BMI) – Sony/ATV Acuff Rose Music (BMI)

The copyright notice for 100% Hank Williams songs is: (example)

I SAW THE LIGHT

100% Hank Williams Sr. (BMI) – Sony/ATV Acuff Rose Music (BMI)

The only thing that changes are the title and © year.

For more interesting reading about Hank Williams

Cusic, Don. *Hank Williams: The Complete Lyrics.*

Escott, Colin with George Merritt and William MacEwen. *Hank Williams: The Biography.*

Flippo, Chet. *Your Cheatin' Heart: A Biography of Hank Williams.*

Florita, Ira and Colin Escott. *Snapshots From the Lost Highway.*

Hemphill, Paul. *Lovesick Blues: The Life of Hank Williams.*

Holmes, Thomas Alan and Roxanne Harde, eds. *Walking the Line: Country Music Lyricists and American Culture.*

Johnson, Rheta Grimsley. *Hank Hung the Moon: And Warmed our Cold, Cold Hearts.*

Williams, Hank and Jimmy Rule. *Hank Williams Tells How to Write Folk and Western Music to Sell.*

Williams, Roger. *Sing a Sad Song: The Life of Hank Williams.*

Index

Song Index